THE HOT AIR FRYER

A Complete Guide On How to Use All Air Fryer Products & Accessories: 55+ Easy To Cook, Fast, Healthy, & Keto-Friendly Recipes for Your Air Fryer.

ANITA GEORGE

Copyright page

Copyright © 2019 by Anita George

All rights reserved. No part of this book may be reproduced or transmitted in any form or by any means, electronic, or mechanical, including photocopying, recording, or by any information storage and retrieval system, without permission from the publisher.

ISBN: 978-1-6976-9047-7

Acknowledgments

A tree can never make a forest; neither can a man be called a team. From this book project, I learned that, indeed, *two heads are better than one.*

My immense gratitude goes to my work partner and spouse-Brown George for his steadfast support in ensuring that I finish this project at the stipulated time. Aside from financial and mental contributions, he helps in handling the home cooking while I'm busy with this project. *He's a darling!*

I have to use this medium and platform to say to Mary Kim, that I appreciate her inputs in helping out with some market researches while compiling this piece. A big thanks go to Oyenekan Oluwafemi, who helped to arrange the index and designing the book cover.

To everyone who has been actively or passively involved in this compilation, I say: I am very grateful! Merci beaucoup!

Copyright page

Copyright © 2019 by Anita George

All rights reserved. No part of this book may be reproduced or transmitted in any form or by any means, electronic, or mechanical, including photocopying, recording, or by any information storage and retrieval system, without permission from the publisher.

ISBN: 978-1-6976-9047-7

Acknowledgments

A tree can never make a forest; neither can a man be called a team. From this book project, I learned that, indeed, *two heads are better than one.*

My immense gratitude goes to my work partner and spouse-Brown George for his steadfast support in ensuring that I finish this project at the stipulated time. Aside from financial and mental contributions, he helps in handling the home cooking while I'm busy with this project. *He's a darling!*

I have to use this medium and platform to say to Mary Kim, that I appreciate her inputs in helping out with some market researches while compiling this piece. A big thanks go to Oyenekan Oluwafemi, who helped to arrange the index and designing the book cover.

To everyone who has been actively or passively involved in this compilation, I say: I am very grateful! Merci beaucoup!

.... **58**

CHAPTER SIX: AIR FRYER SEAFOOD RECIPES.
.... **61**

1. Lemon Garlic Shrimp 63
2. Lemon Pepper Shrimp... 65
3. Garlic Parmesan Shrimp 67
4. Coconut Shrimp with Dipping Sauce 69
5. Bang Bang Fried Shrimp 71
6. Cajun Shrimp.. 73
7. Bacon-Wrapped Shrimp.. 76
8. Popcorn Shrimp... 79
9. Cilantro Lime Shrimp Skewers... 81
10. Lemon Garlic Salmon 84
11. Baked Salmon 86
12. Honey Sriracha Salmon 88
13. Cajun Salmon... 89
14. Asian Salmon 91
15. Salmon and Cauliflower Rice Bowls 93
16. Salmon & Asparagus... 95
17. Tandoori Salmon 97
18. Crumbed Fish... 98
19. Fish Cake Recipe.. 100
20. Grilled Fish Fillet with Pesto Sauce 103
21. Fried Catfish... 105

CHAPTER SEVEN: VEGETABLE RECIPES FOR AIR FRYER **108**

VEGETABLES – AIR FRYER COOKING TIME CHART 109
22. Air Roasted Asparagus...112
23. Buffalo Cauliflower 114
24. Crispy Broccoli 116

Table of Contents

ACKNOWLEDGMENTS .... **II**
TABLE OF CONTENTS .... **III**
INTRODUCTION .... **VII**
CHAPTER ONE: AIR FRYER 101 .... **10**
    MECHANISM OF AIR FRYING APPLIANCES 10
    TRADITIONAL FRIED MEAL VS AIR FRIED MEAL 12
        Know the difference – Vacuum frying, deep-frying, and air frying 12
    ESSENTIAL COMPONENTS OF AN AIR FRYER 14
    ADVANTAGES OF AIR FRYER 16
    DISADVANTAGES OF AIR FRYER 18
    HEALTH BENEFITS AND ADVERSE EFFECTS OF AIR FRYING 19

CHAPTER TWO: AIR FRYER ACCESSORIES .. **22**

CHAPTER THREE: REVIEW OF BEST ECONOMIC PACK AIR FRYERS **30**

CHAPTER FOUR: 15 AIR FRYER TIPS **40**

CHAPTER FIVE: MAINTENANCE AND THE USE OF AIR FRYER **45**
    TIPS ON CLEANING YOUR AIR FRYER 45
        Cleaning the Removable Pieces 46
    AIR FRYER COOKING CHART FOR FROZEN FOOD 48
    TIPS FOR PLACING AND PREPARING FROZEN FOOD IN AN AIR FRYER 50
    CONVERTING ANY RECIPES INTO AN AIR FRYER FRIENDLY RECIPE 51
    FREQUENTLY RELATED QUESTIONS ON AIR FRYER 53
    TROUBLESHOOTING: FIXING COMMON ISSUES THAT COULD ARISE FROM USING YOUR AIR FRYER 56

25. Avocado Fries 118
26. Sweet Potato Fries 120
27. Zucchini, Yellow Squash, and Carrots 122
28. Zucchini Fries 124
29. Zucchini Chips 126
30. Crispy Roasted Brussels Sprouts 128
31. Crispy Kale Chips 130
32. Fried Green Tomatoes 131
33. Honey Roasted Carrots 133
34. Crispy Eggplant Parmesan 134
35. Artichoke Hearts 136
36. Shishito Peppers with Lime 138

CHAPTER EIGHT: POULTRY RECIPES FOR AIR FRYER 140

37. Chicken Wings 'n' Sauce 141
38. Panko Breaded Chicken Parmesan with Marinara Sauce 143
39. Turkey Breast Recipe with Lemon Pepper 145
40. Chicken Fajita Dinner 147
41. Buttermilk Fried Chicken 149
42. Satay Chicken Skewers 151
43. Buffalo Chicken Meatballs 153
44. Honey Mustard Chicken Breasts 155
45. Honey Garlic Chicken Wings 157
46. Turkey Breast 159

CHAPTER NINE: SWEETS RECIPES 161

47. Churros with Chocolate Sauce 162
48. Doughnuts 165
49. Baked Banana Bread 168
50. Cinnamon Apple Chips with Almond Yogurt Dip 170
51. Apple Dumplings 172

52. Pineapple Cake 174
53. Cinnamon Toast 176

CHAPTER TEN: BEEF, PORK AND MUSHROOM RECIPES 178

54. Fried Steak 179
55. Pork Loin 181
56. Beef and Broccoli 183
57. Garlic Mushrooms 184
58. Pork Chop 186
59. Breaded Mushrooms 187

APPENDIX A 190

I. Volumetric Equivalent Table (Liquid) 190
II. Weight conversion table for your recipes 191
III. Length conversion 192

APPENDIX B 193

Dirty Dozen/ Clean Fifteen 193

APPENDIX C 194

Air Fryer Conversion Chart 194
I. Fast Food 194
II. Sweet Recipes Frying 195
III. Potato Air Frying 195

INDEX/RECIPE INDEX 196

Introduction

There is a popular saying in some part of the world, which states:

"Once hunger is taken away from one's problem, poverty is taken away."

It is evident that food is life. As important as food is, it is responsible for the occurrence of numerous health defects and complications, which ranges from digestive, nervous, respiratory disorders, skin problems, obesity, cancer, to mention but a few. Is it enough to stop us from eating what we crave for? A man once said, *"If food is a killer, I rather die from eating what I enjoy than dying from an auto crash that I never envisage."*

Over the years, food scientists have been working immensely to ensure we eat healthily, but most times at the expense of what we crave for. A little child asked me, *"Will you prefer that the stomach is full of a particular food, without having a taste of it?"* Taste gives satisfaction, and sometimes all that is needed to quench hunger is satisfaction.

There is a problem!

In an ideal state, who doesn't like fried food? But we all know how much oil they have. Health-conscious individuals also tend to distance themselves from any oily food. Excessive consumption of greasy food is detrimental.

A way out?

Over the past few years, the term "keto-diet" has gained popularity and become ubiquitous, especially in the US. What is this concept about? Keto here, keto there, is it a type of food? Why the hype?

The ketogenic diet is a low-carb, high-fat diet. Eating more fat and very few carbs put your body in ketosis-a metabolic state where your body burns fat instead of carbs, often leading to a rapid and substantial loss of weight. This seems like good news for obese-risk individuals, right? I guess so. I'm sure you don't want to give up on your crispy fried foods, but they tend to take up so much oil that isn't good for your health. You are not far from a solution. Yes!

Air frying

Air frying is a concept; it is an alternative to other classical frying methods that tends to be unhealthy. Are you familiar with deep frying, and you are wary of the oil consumption you are taking in? It is my utmost pleasure to present to you the best alternative to traditional frying- Air Frying. You need an Air Fryer to air fry your food.

The air fryer can decrease the use of oil in your favorite meal by over 70%. You don't have to be skeptical about this; it is true. It enables you to use little or no oil, and yet the food tastes fantastic.

So, get your fries, chips, chicken wings, and remain well within your calorie objectives every day.

Why do I need this book?

This book, like any other air fryer book, contains recipes that you can try on your own using the air fryer. The uniqueness of this particular one is that it clearly explains the concept of air frying relatively to traditional methods of frying, its health benefits, understanding the components and use of the air fryer kitchen appliance, as well as the maintenance and fixing of minor issues that could arise from its usage. Also, for anyone who has not used an air fryer before, or looking forward to acquiring one, you will get an exclusive guide on making the best purchase.

Aside from the comprehensive, exclusive approach to air frying, there are 55+ easy recipes instructions you can attempt on your own from the comfort of your home. You will also get an exclusive guide to the air fryer accessories that can enable you to get the maximum utility from your air fryer machine.

Lastly, getting yourself an air fryer is possibly the best gift you could give to yourself. It is a way of never compromising on taste again while still keeping your health in check.

Chapter One: Air Fryer 101

An air fryer is an electronic appliance used in the kitchen to cook food in warm air. A mechanical fan makes warm air flowing around the food easier. During this stage, the food is cooked, and a uniform crispy layer is produced around the food. The food can be coated with a thin layer of oil instead of the food products being deep-fried.

The food product under the influence of hot circulating air produces ideal crispiness. They are also faster, as they cook food at half the time it would take, in a regular conventional oven. Most air fryers come with controllable temperature and timer knobs for convenient and customized cooking.

Mechanism of air frying appliances

An air fryer can be best described as a kitchen appliance that cooks with hot air flowing around the food using the convection system. It's a downsized convection oven variant. A mechanical fan circulates hot high-speed air around the food, cooking the food and producing a crispy layer through two steps browning reactions-Maillard and caramelization reaction. In the Maillard reaction, the food is cooked or stir-fried, and then carbohydrates/sugars and proteins react to each other to form Schiff bases, which then form other flavorful compounds, including brown ring compounds comprising one or more nitrogen atoms in the ring, such as pyrazines and pyridines.

The air fryer works to apply heat and initiate the reaction by covering the food in a tiny layer of oil while circulating air is heated to about 400°F (204°C). This enables the appliance to use less than 75% less oil than a traditional deep fryer, and hence browning foods like cheeseburgers, potato chips, French-fries, chicken, seafood, vegetables, etc.

To make cooking more precise, most air fryers have temperature and timer adjustments. Food is boiled in a cooking basket on top of a drip rack. The basket and its contents need to be shaken periodically to guarantee even oil coverage. High-end designs do this by incorporating a food agitator that continuously shakes the food during the process of cooking.

Traditional fried meal vs. air fried meal

The taste of foods cooked by traditional fried and air fried techniques is not identical; as the larger quantity of oil used in conventional frying penetrates the foods (or the coating batter if used) and thus adding its flavor. In specific, if food is only covered in a moist recipe without an appropriate dry coating barrier such as breadcrumbs that are pressed firmly to guarantee adhesion, the mold (or loose crumbs) can be blown off the food by the air fryer fan.

An air fryer is undoubtedly the only kitchen appliance that allows you to binge your favorite meals while maintaining your overall calorie intake significantly lower.

Know the difference – Vacuum frying, deep-frying, and air frying

Vacuum fryer

A vacuum fryer is a deep frying device in a vacuum space. Vacuum fryers are appropriate for handling potatoes of low quality containing higher than normal levels of sugar, as they often have to be processed in spring and early summer before the freshly harvested potatoes are available. With vacuum frying, it is easier to preserve the natural colors and flavors of the completed product. Due to the lower temperatures applied (about 260°F

(~130°C), the formation of suspected carcinogenic acrylamide is much lower than in standard atmospheric fryers with a frying temperature of approximately 340° F (~170°C). Notably, the fat absorption of the products is also reported to be lower than in atmospheric fryers.

Deep frying

Deep frying (also known as deep-fat frying) is a cooking method in which food is submerged in hot fat, most often oil, as opposed to the soft oil used in the frying pan at temperatures typically around 375°F (191°C). A deep fryer or chip pan is usually used for this purpose; a pressure or vacuum fryer can be used for industrial purposes. Typically, deep frying foods cook quickly: cook all sides of the food at the same moment as oil has a high level of heat conductivity.

Deep frying is common around the world, with deep-fried foods representing a significant share of global caloric consumption. Many foods are deep-fried, and deep-frying cultures have evolved, most notably in Africa, Canada, Southern United States, and the United Kingdom, where numerous events and records related to deep-frying food and non-edible products are held.

A popular technique of preparing deep frying food includes adding several layers of batter around the food, such as cornmeal and flour. The surface of it starts to dehydrate after the food is submerged in oil, and it undergoes Maillard reactions that break down sugars and proteins, producing the food's golden brown exterior. It forms a crust once the surface is dehydrated, preventing further oil intake.

Essential components of an air fryer

It is expected that any air fryer has the following detachable parts:

- Cover (main body).
- Basket holder.
- Divider.
- Basket

Fig1.1: An air fryer digital display

Fig 1.2: An air fryer with a non-digital display

The appliance's base is the cover or the primary body that has the operating unit. Above is the basket holder holding the basket for cooking. It has a mechanical fan (this may differ with brands) mounted under it.

Also, there is a cooking basket where the food should be held for cooking. The cooking basket has a foundation in the form of a wire mesh that enables adequate warm air circulation around the food. In addition to the advantages, the system also has a divider that allows you to cook simultaneously distinct food types in the same slot.

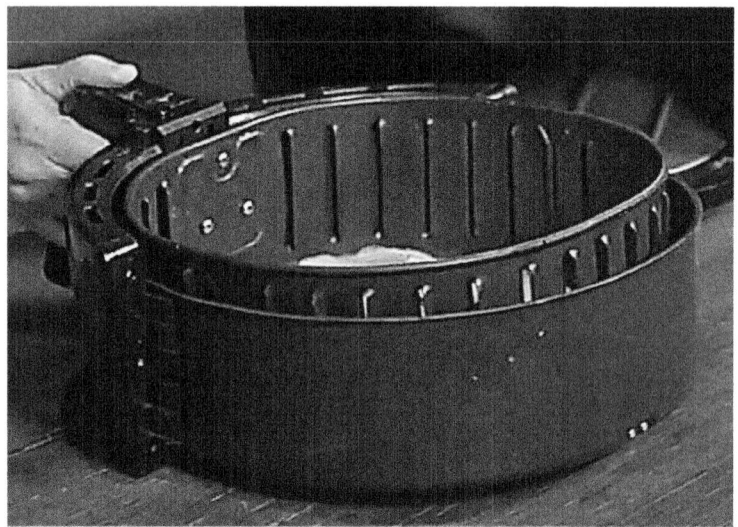

Fig 1.3: The air fryer basket placed in the fry pot, with the hand holding the handle.

Advantages of air fryer

During the cooking process, traditionally deep-fried cooking imparts excessive unnecessary calories to the food through oil absorption. Alternatively, an air fryer prevents all these additional calories and generates healthier versions of the same food maintaining all flavors intact, through the use of little to no oil.

You should invest in a good air fryer if you are a food lover and can't compromise on taste and that satisfying deep-fried crunch but also want to maintain a check on your calorie consumption.

- **Convenience/Ease of use**

The food products need to be monitored minimally. Once they have been covered in the desired/required oil layer, they can be left with a timer laid inside the air fryer and left to cook. Most fryers have the auto-turn off unit with a timer.

In some instances, even oil coverage may require shaking of basket and contents, but it is much more convenient than the traditional stovetop.

- **Health Benefits**

Food cooked in an air fryer requires lesser oil content than conventional cooking, as 2lbs. of French fried or potatoes can be prepared with just 1-2 tablespoons of oil. With mere oil spraying, some dishes can even be cooked. By eliminating the use of fat/oil up to 70% or more, the snack cooked in an air fryer contains much lower calories, making it healthier and more diet-friendly. As air fryers require a fractional volume of the oil needed by deep fryers, people can have a healthier meal with similar flavors and textures.

This is desirable since a person's health can greatly benefit from lowering oil intake. Scientists linked vegetable oil fat intakes to a variety of health conditions, including but not limited to increased risk of heart disease and higher inflammation rates.

- **Safety**

Another significant feature of an air fryer is safety. It eliminates the danger of splashing warm oil over the operator.

Disadvantages of air fryer

Air fryers invaded the kitchen appliance industry with a storm due to the promising claims associated with them. While air fryers add a great deal of convenience, they have some limitations, as well.

- **Limited capacity**

    Air fryers basket has a limited capacity making them unsuitable for a large family-sized meal. Cooking in an air fryer can be a difficult task for more than a couple of adolescents in one batch. However, to rectify this con, air fryers with enhanced cooking capacity are being implemented.

- **Relatively longer cook time**

    Compared to traditional profound frying techniques, air fryers display significantly longer cooking times. To be precise, when compared to deep fryers, an air fryer can take as long as two times the duration.

- **Relatively expensive to a deep fryer**

    Some designs are more priced than standard deep fryers due to the health advantages connected with air fryers. Deep fryers cost as little as $50, while an average air fryer is around $100.

Health benefits and adverse effects of air frying

When used correctly, air fryers offer many healthful benefits:

- Proper usage and recipes can help promote weight loss

Higher intakes of fried foods are directly related to a greater danger of obesity. This is because the fat and calories of deep-fried foods tend to be high. Changing from deep-fried foods to air-fried foods and decreasing periodic consumption of unhealthy oils can contribute to weight loss.

- Air fryers can be safer than deep fryers

Deep-frying food requires a large container full of scalding oil to be heated. This may present a danger to safety. While air fryers get warm, there is no danger that warm oil will spill, splash or accidentally touch the operator.

- Reduces disease risk

Cooking with oil and consuming traditional fried foods regularly has links to many adverse health conditions. Replacing deep frying or cutting down on deep-fried foods can reduce a person's risk of these complications.

Frying food in oil can lead to the development of hazardous compounds such as acrylamide during high-heat cooking techniques, such as deep-frying, acrylamide compound forms in certain ingredients.

Acrylamide may have connections to the growth of some cancers, including endometrial, ovarian, pancreatic, and breast cancer, according to the International Cancer Research Agency. People can reduce the risk of acrylamide in their food by shifting to air frying.

Adverse effects of air fryers

While air fryers have their benefits, they also have their unique collection of adverse effects, including but not limited to, the following:

- **Air frying does not guarantee a complete harmless healthful diet**

Instead of replacing deep-fried foods with air fried foods, an individual should limit their fried food consumption. While air fryers can provide more healthy food choices than deep fryers, a complete limitation of fried food consumption can significantly benefit the health of such a person.

- **Air frying is associated with other harmful compounds aside acrylamides**

While the probability of acrylamide formation is reduced by air fryers, other possibly damaging compounds may still form. Not only does air frying still run the danger of producing acrylamides, but all high-heat cooking with meat can result in polycyclic aromatic hydrocarbons and heterocyclic amines. According to the National Cancer Institute (NCI), these compounds have connections with cancer risk. Although we are still waiting for scientific proofs to explain how air frying correlates with these compounds.

Chapter Two: Air Fryer Accessories

Do not expect an air fryer to come with all the accessories you need to get the best use of it. Air fryer accessories are just like add-ons to the main appliance. Below are some of the accessories for an air fryer that you might need for your next recipe, and their specific functions.

1. Air Fryer Accessories Kits

Air fryer accessory kits in a curated package give the finest range of cooking accessories. The five-piece accessory kit is intended to fit most air fryer products, including the likes of Philips, GoWise, and Power Air Fryer.

The kit comprises a round cake pan with a convenient handle, a multi-purpose cooking rack with optional kabob skewers, a round deep-dish pizza pan, a metal holder rack to maximize cooking surfaces inside your air fryer, and a silicon mat to safeguard countertops and other surfaces from warm pans.

2. Oil Sprayers

Oil sprayers give healthy cooking a distinctive boon. Oil sprayers enable you to use your preferred cooking oil, including cold-pressed oils such as olive oil or grape-seed oil. Unlike purchased shop cooking oil sprays, oil sprayers do not contain aerosols or other chemical propellants, hence making them safer for you and the environment.

There are also accessory kits available to make it even easier to use your oil sprayer. Accessories include a simple bottle refilling twist-on funnel and three stretchable oil identifying bands to label your bottle.

3. Baking Pan

This pan has a diameter of 6.1 inches and a depth of 3 inches. It is intended to fit into a range of air fryer brands from 2.75 to 5.3 quarters. You'll certainly appreciate your air fryer's additional baking pans, even if you've already bought an accessory kit. A la cart baking pan choices include extra dimensions, with various pans allowing you to bake for a crowd.

4. Bundt Pans

Bundt pans in your air fryer will enable you to create beautifully designed cakes. Nordic Ware's 6 Cup Bundt Pan possesses a diameter of 8.5 inches for use in bigger air fryers. Your baked product will be carved into the fluted sides and doughnut-like middle. For simple cleaning, the pan has a non-stick coating and comes in two colors- red poppy or navy.

5. Cake Pans

Cake pans for the air fryer are versatile accessories. Adding specialty cake pans to your air fryer collection, you will be able to bake like a pro. A springform pan, for instance, is accessible in three dimensions—a core of four inches, a round of seven inches, and a round of nine inches. This pan is rated for temperature above 400ºF up to 450ºFahrenheit and is coated for simple cleaning with a non-toxic, BPA-free non-stick layer. To maintain the non-stick lining, hand wash with a soft cloth with a sponge or soft cloth.

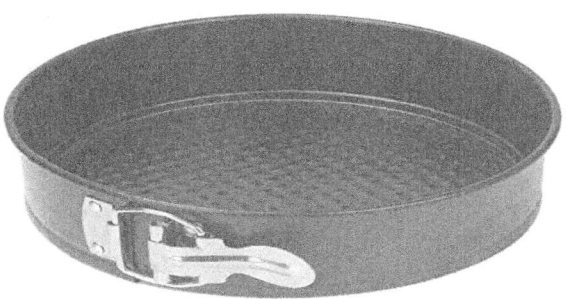

6. Grill Pan

Grill pan perforations allow needed airflow, and the grilling approach generates good products as excess grease drips away. The secure non-stick surface of the dishwasher makes it simple to clean.

7. Cooking Racks

Additional cooking racks boost your air fryer's accessible cooking surface, often enabling you to simultaneously cook two or more food kinds. Specialized cooking racks contribute to your meal preparation versatility.

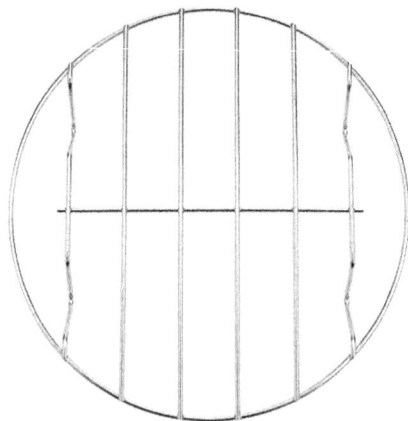

8. Hasselback Potato Slicing Rack

In its concave interior, the potato slicing rack features a sturdy wooden base with two metal prongs to keep your potato safe. The stainless steel cutting guide should be glided into the groove at the base and insert your knife between the guide openings. You can then air-fry your potato air and dress it up with your desirable toppings.

Hasselback potatoes give an added advantage because your baked potato will cook quicker than ever in your air fryer owing to the enhanced surface area and airflow generated by the cutting.

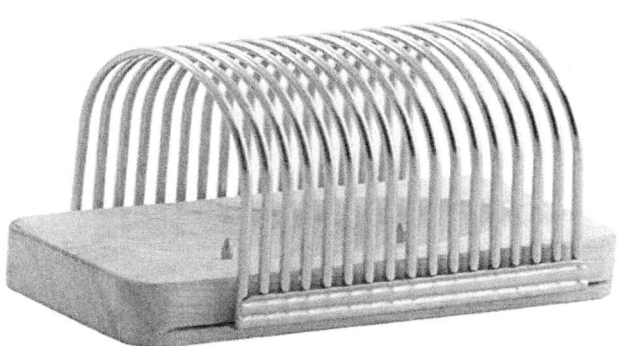

9. Instant Meat and Food Thermometer

This device is a compact, foldable thermometer that can be used with a variety of food products such as meats, casseroles, cakes, sweets, and liquids. Insert the metal probe into the food product and, within 5 seconds, the digital display will show the inner temperature. With a precision range of ±1.8°F, the thermometer is very precise.

The thermometer is suitable for a broad spectrum of cooking apps and can detect temperatures from -49°F to 392°F (-45 to 200°C). For simple reference, a meat safety temperature graph is printed at the back of the thermometer.

10. Parchment Paper Liners

The paper liners provide a non-stick surface, and the ventilation holes included facilitate the flow of air, which is so vital for frying air. The paper liners are 100% natural, non-toxic wood-based paper and can stand up to 20 minutes of severe 450 degrees Fahrenheit temperatures–or longer at reduced temperatures to enable longer cooking times. The liners come in 100 packages.

Parchment air fryer liners are intended for fast and simple cleanup. You can utilize one of the pre-fitted liners instead of taking on the time-consuming job of cutting rolled parchment paper to suit your air fryer. For most air fryers, the 9-inch diameter round liners are a perfect fit.

One extra accessory that I mustn't miss out

Heavy Duty French fry Cutter

In minutes, this heavy-duty cast iron instrument turns potatoes into French fries. The cutter can be installed on a wall or table and is fitted for countertop use with suction cup feet. There are easily accessible replacement components and cutting blades of different dimensions.

Note: For your safety, you can include gloves and tongs to the accessories.

Tip: All of these accessories are easy to get; you can get them from an online market platform or from your kitchen grocery stores.

Chapter Three: Review of Best Economic Pack Air Fryers

These days, air fryers are becoming increasingly common. There are many brands to choose from which the price range varies. Some can be found as little as 75 US Dollars, and some can be as high as over 500 US Dollars.

Some models are unnecessarily overpriced due to some excellent characteristics, while some are reasonably priced with all the critical features. The trick is to differentiate efficiently between what the work is going to do and what is depicted as a fancy addition to your kitchen. This compilation gives an analysis of air fryer appliances that are less than or around the range of 100 US Dollars but with great features.

1. Secura 4 Liters Air Fryer

Description and Pros

- ✓ Spacious 4-liter cooking basket.
- ✓ Knob-style easy controls.
- ✓ The timer can be set maximally to 60 minutes, depending on recipe cook time.

- ✓ The timer possesses a turn-off feature when the cook set-time is up.
- ✓ Powerful 1500-watts power output
- ✓ Functional between 180 to 400°F
- ✓ Complementary skewers, toaster rack, and cookbook
- ✓ Heating and power indicator lights
- ✓ 2-year manufacturer's warranty

<u>Rating</u>: **4.8/5**

2. Ninja Air Fryer AF101 (4 Quarts)

Description/Pros

- ✓ The design of this air fryer is completely BPA[1] free, and the non-stick basket is PFOA[2] free
- ✓ The ceramic-coated non-stick basket and the crisper plate are dishwasher safe, which means they can be washed with little soap and water.

---

[1] *Bisphenol A - It is a colorless solid that is soluble in organic solvents, but poorly soluble in water.*

[2] *Perfluorooctanoic acid (PFOA) is a perfluorinated carboxylic acid produced and used worldwide as an industrial surfactant in chemical processes and as a material feedstock, and is a health concern and subject to regulatory action and voluntary industrial phase-outs.*

- ✓ Besides air frying, it can roast, reheat, and dehydrate.
- ✓ Wide temperature range of 105-400°F
- ✓ Limited 1-year warranty
- ✓ Wattage count of 1550
- ✓ Possess a decently spacious 4-quart cooking basket (it can cook up to 2lbs. of French fries in a single batch)

Cons

The demerit is that it does not come with a cookbook, unlike others.

Rating: **4.6/5**

3. Cosori 3.7 Quart Air Fryer

Description/ Pro

- ✓ It possesses a 5.8-quart spacious dishwasher safe cooking basket
- ✓ Reduced cooking time due to its output power rating of 1500 watt
- ✓ PFOA-free non-stick cooking basket, which is dishwasher safe
- ✓ Sensitive touch controls
- ✓ It can be used between the temperature range of 140 to 400°F

- ✓ It comes with a free cookbook included with 100 recipes
- ✓ 90-days money-back offer
- ✓ 2-year manufacturer's warranty

Cons

It doesn't fit in regular pan cabinets

Rating: **4.5/5**

4. OMORC 6 Quart Air Fryer

Description/ Pros

- ✓ It possesses a spacious capacity of 6 quarts (approximately 5.7 liters), which makes it a good fit family-sized cooking
- ✓ Temperature peaks at 400° F, while timer peaks at 60minutes
- ✓ An enormous power output of 1800 watts
- ✓ Combination of knob-style and touch controls
- ✓ PFOA free non-stick cooking basket (dishwasher safe)
- ✓ It comes with 2-year manufacturer's warranty

Cons

It is a bit slightly bulky

Rating: **4.5/5**

5. GoWISE USA 5.5 Liters Air Fryer

Description/Pros

- Available in a variety of colors- black, red, white, plum and chili
- It comes in 5.8 quarts (5.5 Liter) capacity
- Functional between 180 to 400°F with an auto turn-off feature when the timer goes off.
- It possesses a timer ranges from 1 to 30 minutes
- Output power rating of 1350-watts
- It offers 8 presets to cut hassle
- 1-year manufacturer's warranty
- Vibrant digital display
- An owner's guide with a few recipes for food is included

Cons

The 1-year warranty on the product doesn't cover the baskets, handles and pans as they are warrantied for 30 days only.

Rating: **4/5**

6. Oster Copper-Infused DuraCeramic 3.3-Quart Air Fryer

Description/ Pros

- ✓ Durable ceramic coating over the cooking basket, hence making coating to be highly durable and resilience to flaking
- ✓ Removable parts are dishwasher safe
- ✓ The timer peaks at 30 minutes and the temperature can be up to 400°F
- ✓ Convenient knob-style controls
- ✓ 1-year manufacturer's warranty

Cons

- ✓ The basket capacity is not ideal for cooking family-sized meals
- ✓ No digital display

Rating: **4/5**

7. Tidylife 6 Quart XL Air Fryer

Description/Pros

- ✓ Suitable for a family-sized meal, has it comes in 6.3-quart basket capacity
- ✓ Dishwasher safe cooking basket

- ✓ Consumes lesser counter space
- ✓ 1700 watts output power rating
- ✓ It can be coupled as a grill, sandwich maker, non-stick frying pan and much more
- ✓ It comes with an 18 months manufacturer's warranty

<u>Cons</u>

The control icons look crowded within the display panel

<u>Rating:</u> **4/5**

8. Avalon Bay 3.2 Liters Air Fryer

<u>Description/Pros</u>

- ✓ It comes in a temperature range of 180 and 400°F
- ✓ It possesses a 100% BPA free plastic body
- ✓ It comes in a variety of colors, i.e., black, red, and white.
- ✓ Possess a detachable basket making transferring and food serving easy
- ✓ An output power rating of 1400-watts
- ✓ 30-minute standby timer
- ✓ It comes a non-stick baking dish, a multi-use rack, and a 52-page Avalon Bay cookbook

- ✓ 1-year manufacturer's warranty

Cons

- ✓ A bit heavier
- ✓ Not ideal for bulk cooking
- ✓ Not suitable for individuals who prefer digital controls to knobs

Rating: **3.8/5**

9. Blusmart 3.4 Quart Electric Air Fryer

Description/Pros

- ✓ It can be used for baking, grilling, roasting alongside frying
- ✓ The user interface comes with a compact digital display located right above the power button.
- ✓ The cooking basket is dishwasher safe
- ✓ The timer peaks at 30 minutes and the temperature peaks at 400 °F
- ✓ 60-days money refund offer
- ✓ 1-year manufacturer's warranty

Cons

Not ideal for family-sized meals, as it comes with a 3.4-quart basket capacity

Rating: **3.7/5**

10. Simple Chef 3.5 Quart Air Fryer

Description/Pros

- ✓ This air fryer possess an adjustable cooking temperature range of 180°F to 400 °F
- ✓ It is compact sized
- ✓ It possesses a 3.5 Liter cooking capacity
- ✓ 100% BPA free plastic body
- ✓ Dishwasher safe cooking basket
- ✓ Output power rating of 1400-watts
- ✓ 15-page recipe book included
- ✓ 2-year manufacturer's warranty

Cons

Not ideal for bulk cooking

Rating: **3.5/5**

One of the most notable brands of air fryer in the market is the Philips HD9641/96 Air fryer, which cost over $250.

Breville BOV900BSS Convection and Air Fry Smart Oven Air is another expensive air fryer that has 1 cubic foot of interior space. It is ideal for large cooking, and cost about $400.

Chapter Four: 15 Air Fryer Tips

1. Oil your air fryer basket

Even if your food doesn't need oil, ensure that the air fryer basket is minimally greased. I grease a little bit of oil on the bottom grates by rubbing or spraying. This will guarantee that your food will not stick.

2. Do not use aerosol spray cans in your air fryer

In many Air Fryer baskets, aerosol spray cans are known to cause chipping. On most baskets, the aerosol cans have harsh agents that don't mesh with the coating. Investing in a good quality oil bottle is best.

3. Don't overcrowd the basket

If you want to make your fried food crispy, make sure you don't overcrowd the basket. Your food will be prevented from crisping and browning, when you place too much food in the basket. It is better to cook your food in batches or invest in a bigger air fryer to make sure this doesn't occur.

4. Shake the basket when cooking fries and similar items.

It is important to shake the basket every few minutes to ensure even cooking when air frying smaller items, such as chicken wings, French fries, and similar items. Sometimes, you can use a pair of silicone kitchen tongs instead of shaking to flip larger items over. The air fryer will temporarily pause once you open the basket to shake, but will resume cooking at the same temperature once you return the basket.

5. Spray halfway through cooking

I found the best crisp on most foods is spraying with oil halfway through cooking. I tend to wait and spray midway through cooking unless it's like fatty meats that don't need spraying. It is necessary to spray coated food items.

6. Adjust the temperature for certain food

Sometimes it can be tempting to crank the heat to let the air fryer run but be cautious as some products can dry out rapidly. You can to go down 30 degrees and cut the time by around 20% relative to your oven time/temperature. For instance, if you are cooking brownies in the oven for 20 minutes at 360°F, cut the air fryer degrees to 330°F and cook for about 16 minutes.

7. Water stops white smoke in the bottom

Do not be surprised if you see some white smoke flying out of the unit when you are cooking sticky food in your air fryer. To fix it, pour a little water (around 2 tablespoons) into the basket bottom. It will prevent the smoke, and your food will continue to cook. You can also put a slice of bread in the bottom of the unit to soak any grease when preparing products like bacon that can sputter a lot of greases.

8. Take an extra precaution of small light items in the air fryer

Every fryer system comes with a strong fan unit. This leads to heavier weighed products being swept into the fan, which can be hazardous.

9. Do not hesitate to use oil on your foods for the air fryer

I like using oil on some foods to make them crisp, but some foods don't need it. You probably don't need the oil if your food has some fat (dark meat chicken, ground beef, fatty pieces of meat, etc.). you can use oil on vegetables and any battered seafood.

10.   Preheat your air fryer if you have to

Although this practice is not necessary, it is a prevalent practice to preheat any cooking component. Most air fryer manufacturers indicate that to guarantee even cooking, the air fryer should be preheated. Sometimes I do it, sometimes I don't do it, and my food is still delicious. If you do not have a preheat environment in your air fryer, merely switch it to the required temperature and enable it to run for about 3-5 minutes before putting your food.

Pre-heating is very necessary when your air fryer cannot reach your desired temperature, but aside that, it is not.

Manufacturers' Tips

11. Usually, smaller ingredients involve a slightly shorter preparation time compared to bigger ingredients.

12. A greater quantity of ingredients needs only a slightly longer preparation period; a lower quantity of ingredients needs only a slightly shorter preparation period.

13. Halfway through the preparation period, shaking smaller ingredients optimizes the outcome and can help avoid uneven fried ingredients.

14. Add some oil for a crispy result to the fresh potatoes. In the air fryer, fry your ingredients within a few minutes of adding the oil.

15. Any snacks that can be prepared in the oven can also be made in the air fryer.

⚠ Caution

- The appliance should always be unplugged after use.
- After use, allow about thirty minutes before you clean or handle it.
- Make sure the ingredients are golden-yellow instead of dark or brown in this appliance and remove the remains from burnt.
- Do not prepare very greasy ingredients in the air fryer, such as sausages.
- Do not use wax papers in the air fryer, use aluminum foil instead if necessary.

Chapter Five: Maintenance and the Use of Air Fryer

Tips on cleaning your air fryer

You might be considering cleaning your air fryer appliance, but for whatever reason or reasons, consider cleaning your air fryer when any of the following occurs:

- If your food is not cooking as even as you desire or you find it sticking to the cooking basket, cleaning the components should fix this.

- When you notice a lot of smoke emanating from the fryer, then the heating element or fan may need to be cleaned.

- When you perceive an unpleasant smell in your kitchen, and you are not sure what it is, ensure to check your air fryer power cable and clean the components if dirty.

- Whenever you discover the cooking tray or basket to be sticky or grimy, ensure to clean it immediately. (We will discuss that shortly)

Cleaning the Removable Pieces

To ensure the longevity of your air fryer, you need to keep it clean. Some of my friends invite me to their homes to clean their air fryer for them; I tell them it isn't a big deal at all.

⚠️ Below is a guide believed to be applicable to most air fryer in the market today, therefore remember to consult your air fryer instruction manual for more on cleaning guidelines.

Let's begin:

A. The removable piece of an air fryer

The removable pieces of the air fryer are the easiest to keep clean. Follow the tips below, and you are good to go.

- Unplug the air fryer from the power source and remove all the pieces you can. Most parts are detachable, don't fidget!
- Check your fryer's manual to see if some of your air fryer components are dishwasher safe. If it not the case, rinse the basket, grill tray, and other removable pieces with warm water.
- Add some dishwashing liquid and let them soak for 20 minutes.
- Clean the components using a soft-bristle brush.
- Dry completely with paper towels and assemble them back.

B. Cleaning the Outside

Cleaning the outer part of your air fryer shouldn't be as frequent as the interior part. Once in a while, it might be due for a cleaning, and there are no technicalities in doing so at all.

Below is a simple stepwise guide:

- Start by unplugging the air fryer from the power source
- Using a damp cloth, wipe down the exterior of the appliance
- Dry thoroughly with a paper towel.

C. Cleaning the Fan Component and Heater

The fan and the heating element component may be difficult to reach, but the good side is that they rarely require cleaning. If you can reach them, ensure to clean them out as regularly as possible using the procedure below:

- Start by unplugging the air fryer from the power source
- Proceed by using a soft bristle scrub brush
- Scrub the heating coil with warm water gently (Avoid using soap)
- Dry the heating coil with a paper towel

- Use a small, thin wire brush to scrape off any dust or food particles that might have stuck into it.

⚠️ Do not use water on the fan component, and do not use hard bristles on the heating element,

Air fryer cooking chart for frozen food

You can use cooking charts to get an estimate of how long and at what temperature specific food should be cooked when cooking with an air fryer. As there isn't a universal size for chicken breasts all over the world, the cooking chart may need to be adjusted depending on the size of your chicken breast or whatever it may be you are cooking, so you don't stand the risk of eating uncooked food, particularly poultry.

On the next page is a cooking chart for frozen food in the air fryer.

Air fryer cooking chart for frozen food items

Type	Cooking Time (minutes)	Temperature (°F)	Temperature (°C)
Frozen Burritos	10	400	200
Frozen Chicken Breast	20-25	*390(preheat)	190
Frozen Chicken Strips	12	390	200
Frozen Chicken Tenders	10	400	200
Frozen Chicken Wings	9	400	200
Frozen Corn Dogs	10	400	200
Frozen Fish Fingers	8	360	180
Frozen French Fries (Thick)	18	400	200
Frozen French Fries (Thin)	14	400	200
Frozen Hamburgers	13	360	180
Frozen Mozzarella Sticks	18	400	200
Frozen Onion Rings	8-10	400	200
Frozen Pizza Rolls	7	380	190
Frozen Sausage Rolls	13	360	180
Frozen Shrimp	9	400	200

*When cooking frozen food like chicken breast, It is recommended that you either preheat the air fryer for 5 minutes at 320°F(160°C) before you start cooking it at the recommended temperature.

Tips for placing and preparing frozen food in an air fryer

The air fryer seems like a simple appliance to use, even for the fact it doesn't come with guidelines for every situation, but the following tips will help when preparing frozen food in an air fryer.

- Make sure you are generous with the space you offer each piece of food items when cooking frozen food in an air fryer. You can prevent them from sticking to each other by spreading them out as much as possible.

- You should shake the basket halfway to prevent the food from sticking to the basket.

- When you finish shaking the basket, make sure that the food is separated again before putting it in the air fryer once again. I'm sure you won't have these issues if you own an XL air fryer. Some air fryers are more spacious than the others, but you have to use what you have got. There are accessories to solve your problem if you don't own one, so you don't have to worry.

- When your frozen food isn't breaded or wrapped, there is a risk of losing the texture of the food when it is air fried. To prevent the food from altering its texture, you need to moisturize the frozen food if it isn't wrapped or breaded before cooking it in the air fryer. This is achieved by adding a sauce or dressing to your frozen food before cooking so that some moisture is present when cooking. The sauce keeps the meat from having a dry texture and also improves its flavors.

Converting any recipes into an air fryer friendly recipe

Most food packages don't have instructions for air fryers yet, so, as the owner of the air fryer, you have the task to convert the recipes to make them more suitable for air fryers. You are advised not to follow the cooking instructions for microwave or an oven when cooking in an air fryer because the outcome is most probably going to be awful.

You can search for an online calculator that transforms your recipes from conventional ovens to air fryers. It's simple, take the traditional recipe (cooking instructions) and offer the calculator the data it needs. It's going to inform you immediately what you need to tweak to cook a dish with an air fryer.

It's a very helpful device, you're going to get the hang of it after a while, and you're going to be able to transform your recipes into an air-fryer compatible recipe.

Here is a list of some tips to get the best of output from your air frying appliance.

- ✓ Shake the basket midway into cooking to ensure that the food is evenly cooked. It is crucial to expose all sides of the food to the air fryer's warm air.

- ✓ Don't stack the frozen foods on top of each other; alternatively, offer them space, so the air flows through. Stacking the foods will inhibit thorough cooking.

- ✓ Take into account the air fryer's size and power output, as larger air fryers are often stronger than smaller air fryers with reduced wattage. The distinction between them is comparatively tiny, but it may be helpful to be conscious of it.

Frequently Related Questions on Air Fryer

Q: Can you cook frozen vegetables in an air fryer?

Yes, frozen vegetables can be cooked in an air fryer. Sprinkle on the vegetables your favorite spices, and you have a very good, low-calorie snack. Follow the packaging directions and use the same temperature, half the cooking time rule.

Cooking vegetables in a typical air fryer makes them more delicious and easier for kids who do not generally consume enough greens to eat.

Q: What kind of meal can you prepare with an air fryer?

The list is exhaustive, frozen foods, desserts, snacks, croissants, and many more recipes do very well in an air fryer. If you want your vegetables cooked in different ways, then an air fryer is a good fit for you, as it can help you roast them to that crisp but tender texture you crave for.

Q: Should I preheat my air fryer?

The air fryer does not have to preheat, unlike a conventional oven. You'd cut the cooking time down very little by preheating the air fryer. You can go ahead and put your ingredients in the air fryer and press start unless there seems to be a particular reason to preheat the air fryer. If the recipe cooking instruction tells you to preheat, then do so freely.

Q: Do I need to use cooking oil in preparing my recipe?

Yes! You can't rule that out. The good thing about an air fryer is that it enables you to cook food smoothly with a spray of oil, or with as little as a tablespoon of oil depending on the food. Notably, some foods do not require oil for cooking, as their fat content is enough to do the cooking. Just ensure you use healthy cholesterol-free oil.

Q: Is air fryer worth it?

Aside from the fact that it enables you to cook most of your recipes with little or no oil, it is a fast way of cooking as well. It doesn't take as much space as most of your kitchen appliances.

Q: Is an oven better than an air fryer?

They are both good. It depends on what you are using it for. They both have their limitations, as well. An air fryer cooks food faster, portable in size, and allowing different cooking techniques to achieve quite a number of delicacies, but with a smaller food size capacity. The oven allows cooking in a larger portion, but it requires a dedicated space in your kitchen as compared to the air fryer.

Q: Why do air fryers smoke so much?

It is quite normal, but it shouldn't be excessive. One of the possible reasons for excessive smoking is cooking foods with high-fat content; therefore, the fat tends to drain. This can be rectified by suspending the cooking briefly and draining the excess fat.

Q: Can I use any kind of oil spray for my air fryer?

While some air fryer specifies the use of cooking spray or olive oil, some suggest others. Therefore check your manufacturer's instructions for clarity.

Troubleshooting: Fixing common issues that could arise from using your air fryer

Problem	Possible Causes	Solution
The air fryer not working	The appliance is not well plugged.	Ensure you put the mains plug in an earthed wall socket.
	Air fryer timer not set	Set the timer to the required cooking time to kick-off the appliance
White smoke oozing out of the air fryer	The ingredients you are cooking is greasy (Frying greasy ingredients in the air fryer results in a large amount of oil leaking into the pan.	Add little water into pan to minimize the smoke.
	The pan contains grease from the previous cooking.	Ensure to clean your cooking pan after each use.
Cooking pan not sliding into the air fryer appropriately.	The ingredients are too much in the basket.	Ensure that you do not overfill the basket, the lesser, the better. You can cook your food in batches instead.
	The basket not correctly placed.	Gently push the basket down into the pan until you hear a click sound.

		There might be an obstruction between the pan and handle of the baking tray.	In a horizontal position, push the handle, so it does not stick out on top of the basket.
The ingredients in the air fryer are unevenly fried.		Failure to shake Ingredients halfway through the stipulated cooking period.	Food recipes that lie on top of each other need to be shaken periodically during the cooking time.
The ingredients fried are not well cooked.		The quantity of ingredients in the basket is larger than its holding capacity.	Put ingredients in batches into the basket. Smaller batches are fried more evenly than larger ones.
		The temperature set is much lower than it should be.	Turn the temperature control knob to the temperature as given by the recipe instruction.
		The preparation time is shorter than it ought to be.	Turn the timer knob to the required preparation time, as instructed in your recipe cookbook.

THE

AIR FRYER

RECIPES

All recipes instructions in this section are to be used with the air fryer only.

Enjoy!

Important Notice

1. Read through the recipe guide carefully before attempting to prepare any meal from the recipe book to avoid getting stuck.

2. The cook time given in the recipe instructions are adjustable, do not be limited to it, as it can be adjusted. Since air fryers come in different brands and sizes, there is always room for slight differences. Another reason why cook time is flexible is that larger (thicker) recipes are expected to cook longer than smaller (thinner) ones. Apparently, you need to adjust cook time appropriately. I always advise that if the recipe instruction states 10 minutes cook time, and after 10 minutes, you discover that you're not pleased with the crispness, you can continue cooking a little longer. But ensure you don't over-stock the air fryer.

3. In a case where a sauce is mentioned to accompany a recipe, it is not mandatory to go with such sauce if you have a desirable alternative sauce.

4. The accuracy of the nutritional information is not guaranteed. You might need to consult your nutritionist to help you evaluate the nutrition value appropriately.

Alternatively, you can use some nutritional facts online calculator, which usually requires you to provide the ingredients.

5. Recipes from air fryer are not 100% healthy. It is only healthier than most classical frying methods.

6. Temperature conversion from the Fahrenheit scale to Celsius degree scale given in the recipes are approximate values. For instance, 400°F in the Celsius scale is 204°C, but we use 200°C, this is because air fryers that come with Celsius temperature scale peak at 200°C.

Chapter Six: Air Fryer Seafood Recipes.

A shrimp has high protein content but small food energy content. Depending on the preparation technique, a shrimp-based meal is also an important source of cholesterol, with a concentration between 110 mg to 251 mg per 100 g of shrimp.

However, shrimp consumption is regarded as healthy for the circulatory system because the absence of important saturated fat concentrations in shrimps implies that the high cholesterol content in shrimps effectively improves the LDL-to-HDL cholesterol ratio and reduces triglycerides.

Most of the recipes in the book under this section require 1 pound (1lb.) of shrimp, but shrimp come in various sizes, so ensure to pick the right size for this recipe.

Shrimp are classified by size. The number refers to the number of shrimp in a pound. The higher the number, the smaller each shrimp is. Below is a guide:

16/20 – extra jumbo

21/25 – jumbo

26/30 – extra large

31/35 – large

36/40 – medium large

41/50 – medium

51/60 – small

Buy frozen shrimp and defrost as required. Most shrimps get frozen in shops so you can purchase it frozen and defrost it, as you need to make it as fresh as possible — thaw overnight in the refrigerator to defrost shrimp.

Quick Note: Air fryer temperatures can vary depending on the manufacturer and model, so it is essential and expected that you always check your food to check if it is cooked enough for your preference, and adjust the cooking time as needed.

1. Lemon Garlic Shrimp

Cuisine: air fryer, seafood

Prep Time	10 minutes
Cook Time	15 minutes
Total Time	25 minutes
Servings	4

Ingredients

- 2 lbs. raw shrimp, peeled deveined,
- 1 teaspoon vegetable oil or spray, to coat shrimp
- ½ teaspoon garlic powder
- Salt- to taste
- Black pepper- taste
- 2 lemon wedges
- minced parsley

Instructions

1. Toss the shrimp with the oil (In a bowl).
2. Add garlic powder, pepper, and salt and then toss to evenly coat the shrimp.
3. Add shrimp to the air fryer basket in one layer.
4. Air fry the mixed recipe at 400°F (200°C) for about 10-15 minutes, gently shaking and flipping halfway,

depending on the shrimp size (about 4 minutes for smaller shrimps, 6 minutes for larger shrimps).

5. Transfer the air-fried shrimp into a bowl,

6. **Optional:** Squeeze lemon juice on top, sprinkle parsley, and chili flakes.

Serving suggestion: Serve the shrimp on a salad, or with anything you want.

Nutritional Informational

Calories: 225Cal | Carbohydrates: 12.2g | Fat: 8.4g| Saturated Fat: 1.0g| Cholesterol: 250mg| Dietary Fiber: 5.5g| Protein: 27.9g

2. Lemon Pepper Shrimp

Prep Time	5 minutes
Cook Time	10 minutes
Total Time	15 minutes
Servings	2

Ingredients

- 12 oz. uncooked shrimp (peeled and deveined)
- 2 lemon (sliced)
- 1 lemon juiced
- 1 tablespoon olive oil
- 1 teaspoon lemon pepper
- 1/4 teaspoon garlic powder
- 1/4 teaspoon paprika

Instructions

1. Preheat the air fryer to 400°F (200°C).

2. Combine lemon juice, lemon pepper, olive oil, paprika, and garlic powder in a bowl.

3. Add shrimp and toss until it is well coated with the prepared mixture.

4. Place shrimp in the air fryer and cook for about 7 to 10 minutes, when it must have turned pink and firm. Serve with lemon slices.

Serving suggestion: Add salad.

Nutritional Informational

Calories: 210Cal| Carbohydrates: 12.2g| Fat: 8.4g| Saturated Fat: 1.0g| Cholesterol: 250mg| Dietary Fiber: 6g| Protein: 28.9g

3. Garlic Parmesan Shrimp

Prep Time	1-2 hrs.
Cook Time	10 minutes
Servings	4

Ingredients

- 2 lb. shrimp - deveined and peeled
- 2 tablespoon olive oil
- 2 teaspoon salt
- 2 teaspoon fresh cracked pepper
- 2 tablespoon lemon juice
- 12 cloves garlic (diced)
- 1 cup grated parmesan cheese
- 1/2 cup diced cilantro or parsley, to garnish (optional)

Instructions

1. Preheat the air fryer to 350°F (180°C) for 5 minutes.

2. In a bowl, coat shrimp in olive oil and lemon juice, season with salt and pepper, and garlic.

3. Cover the resulting mixture with plastic wrap and refrigerate for at least an hour, depending on the level of lemon flavor you desire.

4. Toss parmesan cheese into the bowl with shrimp.

5. Add shrimp to the basket, and cook at 350°F (180°C) for 10 minutes.

6. Serve immediately!

Nutritional Informational

Calories: 150Cal | Carbohydrates: 4.0g | Fat: 6g| Saturated Fat: 2.0g| Unsaturated Fat: 3.2g | Cholesterol: 165mg| Protein: 22g

4. Coconut Shrimp with Dipping Sauce

Course: Appetizer, Cuisine: American

Prep Time	10 minutes
Cook Time	10 minutes
Total Time	20 minutes
Servings	2

Ingredients

- ¼ cup Panko Breadcrumbs
- ¼ teaspoon black pepper
- ½ cup All-Purpose Flour
- ½ cup of shredded coconut (unsweetened)
- 1 lb. raw shrimp (peeled and deveined with tail on)
- 1 teaspoon salt
- 2 eggs (beaten)
- Oil for spraying

Instructions

1. Clean and dry shrimps
2. Place shrimp in a layer in the air fryer basket that has been oiled.

3. Spray the shrimp with little oil and then close the air fryer basket, and allow cooking for 4 minutes.

4. After 4 minutes, open the air fryer basket and flip over the shrimp. Spray shrimp once again, close air fryer basket, and cook for additional 5 minutes.

5. Remove shrimp from the basket and serve immediately.

Serving Suggestion: Serve with Thai Sweet Chili Sauce.

Nutritional Informational

Calories: 290Cal | Carbohydrates: 17.0g | Fat: 10g| Saturated Fat: 6.0g| Cholesterol: 360mg| Protein: 27.2g | Fiber: 2.3g

5. Bang Bang Fried Shrimp

Course: dinner and lunch; Cuisine: American

Prep Time	10 minutes
Cook Time	15 minutes
Total Time	25 minutes
Servings	2

Ingredients

- 1 egg white
- 1lb. raw medium shrimp (peeled and deveined)
- 1 tablespoon sesame seeds
- 1 teaspoon paprika
- 1/2 cup all-purpose flour
- 1/2 cup diced green onions
- 1/4 cup sweet chili sauce
- 2 tablespoon Sriracha
- 3/4 cup panko bread crumbs
- Bang Bang Sauce
- Cooking spray
- Chicken Seasoning to taste (use any chicken seasoning you desire)
- salt and pepper to taste

☞ *Instructions*

1. Preheat air fryer to 375°F (190°C).
2. Add the seasoning to the shrimp.
3. Place the flour, egg whites, and panko bread crumbs in three bowls, respectively.
4. Lightly dredge shrimp in flour, then dip in the bowl containing the egg whites, and lastly, dip in the panko bread crumbs until the shrimp is uniformly coated.
5. Arrange shrimp in a single layer into the air fryer basket and spray.

⚠️ Spraying shrimp directly could lead to the panko bread crumbs jumping off the uniformly coated shrimp. Keep a distance before spraying.

6. Cook for 5 minutes. Open the basket and flip the shrimp to the other side — Cook for an additional 5 minutes or until you are satisfied with the crispness.
7. Bang Bang Sauce: Combine all of the sauce ingredients in a small bowl. Mix thoroughly until smooth

Serving suggestion: Garnish shrimp with diced green onions and sesame seeds.

Nutritional Informational

Calories: 242Cal | Carbohydrates: 54g | Fat: 25g| Saturated Fat: 4.0g| Cholesterol: 65mg| Sugar: 10.9g | Fiber: 2g

6. Cajun Shrimp

Course: Dinner; Cuisine: American, Cajun

Prep Time	20 minutes
Cook Time	10 minutes
Total Time	30 minutes
Servings	4

Ingredients

- 1 tablespoon Cajun or Creole seasoning
- 1/4 teaspoon kosher salt
- 2 tablespoons olive oil
- 1 lb. of extra-jumbo shrimp (cleaned and peeled)
- 6 oz. fully cooked Chicken Andouille sausage (sliced)
- 1 large red bell pepper (seeded and cut into thin 1-inch pieces)

- 8 ounces medium yellow squash (1) (sliced into 1/4-inch thick half-moons)

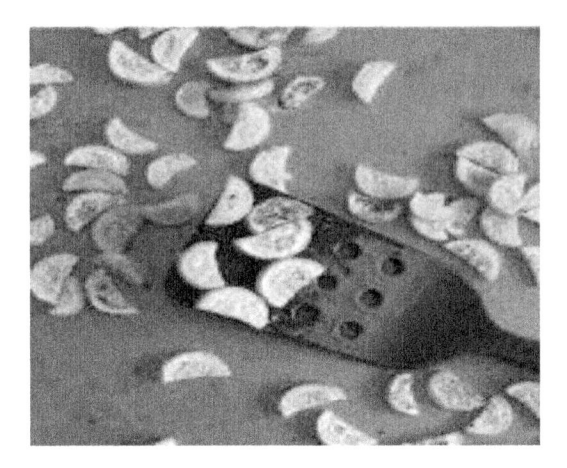

- 8 ounces medium zucchini (1)

  (8 ounces, sliced into 1/4-inch thick half-moons)

☞ *Instructions*

1. Combine the Cajun seasoning and shrimp in a large bowl, toss to coat the shrimp.

2. Add the bell peppers, sausage, squash, salt, and zucchini and toss with the oil.

3. Preheat the air fryer to 400°F (200°C).

4. Put the shrimp and vegetables into the air fryer basket and cook for 8 minutes, shaking the basket 2 to 3 times during this interval (In case of smaller baskets, cook in 2 batches).

5. *Once the shrimp is cooked, repeat step (4) with the remaining shrimp and veggies (in the case of multiple batches).

6. Once both batches are cooked, take the first-set back to the air fryer and cook again for 2 minutes.

Nutritional Informational

Calories: 280Cal | Carbohydrates: 8.0g | Fat: 14g| Saturated Fat: 2.0g| Cholesterol: 215mg| Protein: 28g | Fiber: 2g

7. Bacon-Wrapped Shrimp

Prep Time	20 minutes
Cook Time	10 minutes
Total Time	30 minutes
Servings	2

Ingredients

- 1 cup cocktail sauce
- 1 jalapeño fresh pepper (seeded and cut into thin strips)
- 1lb bacon (12 slices cut in half
- 1lb raw shrimp (peeled with tails on)
- 1/4 cup chipotle peppers in [3]adobo sauce (chopped fine)

Instructions

1. At 390ºF, preheat the air fryer for 5 minutes, while you prepare the shrimp.

   Wrapping the Bacon

---

[3] Adobo sauce is made from chili powder, herbs, sugar, vinegar, and garlic

2. Place a shrimp and a thin slice of jalapeño pepper on one end of the shrimp.

3. Roll the shrimp in the bacon by wrapping it gently but tightly.

4. For 10-15minutes, chill the shrimp to set the bacon.

Making the Chipotle Cocktail Dipping Sauce

5. Mix the chopped chipotle peppers and cocktail sauce

6. Chill until ready to serve with the bacon-wrapped shrimp.

Air Fry the Shrimp

7. Place the shrimp in the basket at 390°F (~200°C) and cook for 5 minutes

8. Flip the shrimp over and air fry for another 5 minutes to ensure uniformity

9. Serve with Chipotle Cocktail Sauce!

Key Note:

- Make sure you're using the shell on raw shrimp.
- Do not use the deveined shrimp.
- Before cooking in the air fryer, chill the bacon-wrapped shrimp in the fridge. This helps to keep the bacon-wrapped and prevents the shrimp from overcooking.

- Ensure to serve the meal on a warm plate or keep the cooked ones in a warm oven until you are done frying the subsequent batches.

Nutritional Informational

Calories: 460Cal | Carbohydrates: 14.0g | Fat: 25g| Saturated Fat: 7g|Sugar: 5g | Cholesterol: 175mg| Protein: 35g | Fiber: 1g

8. Popcorn Shrimp

Prep Time	20 minutes
Cook Time	20 minutes
Total Time	40 minutes
Servings	4

Ingredients

- 12 oz. large shrimp (peeled and deveined)
- 1 egg
- 1 cup panko bread crumbs
- Nonstick cooking spray
- 1/2 teaspoon paprika
- 1/2 teaspoon onion powder
- 1/4 cup all-purpose flour
- 1/4 teaspoon salt
- 1/8 teaspoon ground black pepper

Instructions

1. In a large bowl, place shrimp, sprinkle flour over the top and toss until shrimp are evenly coated in flour.

2. Beat egg in a separate bowl, and combine panko bread crumbs, onion powder, paprika, salt, and pepper in another bowl.

3. Dip each flour-coated shrimp in the egg bowl.

4. Toss the shrimp in panko mixture, and place on a baking sheet, and allow resting for 5 minutes.

5. Preheat air fryer to 400°F (200°C) for 5 minutes.

6. Arrange about half of the shrimp in the basket — Mist the top of each shrimp with cooking spray.

7. Cook shrimp for 5 minutes, check and flip shrimp over, and cook 4 minutes more. Repeat with the remaining other 1/2 of the shrimp.

Nutritional Informational

Calories: 180Cal | Carbohydrates: 25g | Fat: 2.8g| Saturated Fat: 9g|Sugar: 5g | Cholesterol: 175mg| Protein: 20g | Fiber: 0.3g

9. Cilantro Lime Shrimp Skewers

Course: Appetizer, Dinner; Cuisine: American

Prep Time	20 minutes
Cook Time	10 minutes
Total Time	30 minutes
Servings	4

Ingredients

- tablespoon of chopped cilantro (fresh coriander leaves)
- Juice of extracted from 1 lemon
- Salt to taste
- 1/2 lb. raw shrimp (peeled and deveined)
- 1/2 teaspoon garlic purée
- 1/2 teaspoon ground cumin
- 1/2 teaspoon paprika

Instructions

1. Soak 5 wooden skewers for 15-20 minutes before use.
2. Preheat air fryer to 350°F (177°C).

3. In a bowl, mix lemon juice, cumin, garlic, paprika, and salt.
4. Add shrimp and stir to coat with the mixture evenly.
5. Thread shrimp onto the skewers.
6. Place skewers in the air fryer and ensure that they are not touching each other.
7. Cook for 5-8 minutes, turning skewers halfway through the cooking time.
8. After cooking, transfer the shrimp to a plate and serve with the chopped cilantro (fresh coriander leaves), and add extra lime slices (if you wish).

Grill Instructions:

1. Preheat the grill, and oil the grill plate
2. Put the shrimp on a griddle on the hot grill.
3. Cook for 2-3 minutes on each side until they are cooked through.
4. Transfer to a plate and serve.

Note:

- You are permitted to vary the spices and herbs to suit your taste.

- Ensure that the skewers fit your air fryer. If you have a longer skewer, you can cut it to about 6.5 inches or on the size of your air fryer.

Nutritional Informational

Calories: 65Cal | Carbohydrates: 25.2g | Fat: 2.9g| Saturated Fat: 8g | Cholesterol: 145mg| Protein: 12g |

10. Lemon Garlic Salmon

Prep Time	5 minutes
Cook Time	14 minutes
Total Time	19 minutes
Servings	4

Ingredients

- 1 lemon, sliced into thin rounds
- 1 teaspoon celtic sea salt
- 1 teaspoon fresh cracked pepper
- 1 teaspoon lemon juice
- 2 tablespoon olive oil
- 2 teaspoon garlic powder
- 2 teaspoon Italian herbs
- 6 oz. salmon filets (x4)

Instructions

1. In a large bowl, sprinkle olive oil and lemon juice over salmon, rub to make sure the salmon filets are evenly coated.

2. Season with pepper, salt, and Italian herbs.

3. Arrange salmon fillets in the air fryer basket, and make sure there is minimal contact.

4. Arrange the lemon slices on and around the salmon in the air fryer basket.

5. Set air fryer to 400°F(200°C) and cook accordingly:

    Salmon with a little bit of red in the middle requires 10 minutes;

    Salmon with no red in the middle requires 12 minutes cook time;

    Thicker salmon filets require 14 minutes of cook time.

6. Serve and enjoy!

Nutritional Informational

Calories: 462Cal | Carbohydrates: 13g | Fat: 28g| Saturated Fat: 5g|Sugar: 2g | Cholesterol: 110mg| Protein: 40g | Fiber: 2g

11. Baked Salmon

Prep Time	10 minutes
Cook Time	10 minutes
Total Time	20 minutes
Servings	2

Ingredients

- 6 oz. salmon fillets x 2 (skin and bones removed)
- Cooking spray or 1 teaspoon olive oil
- kosher salt
- black pepper

Instructions

1. Rinse and pat dry the salmon. Lightly coat with oil or cooking spray.
2. Season both sides with salt and pepper.
3. Place salmon in the basket. Air fry at 360°F (180°C) for about 8-10 minutes, depending on how you want it.
4. Gently press the salmon to check if it is ready. (It is done when it is firm, the firmer it is, the better).

Quick Note

- If you are using a larger air fryer, the recipe cook time might vary, so adjust accordingly.

- If your air fryer isn't large enough, don't double the recipes. You might have to cook in batches.

- The cook time for the first batch will take longer if the air fryer is not pre-heated before the cooking.

12. Honey Sriracha Salmon

Prep Time	20 minutes
Cook Time	12 minutes
Total Time	32 minutes
Servings	4

Ingredients

- 2 tablespoon soy sauce
- 1 cup honey
- 1/2 cup Sriracha
- 1 1/2 lbs. salmon (cut into 2 fillets, skin on)

Instructions

1. In a bowl, mix the honey, sriracha, and soy sauce.
2. Take half of the sauce for dipping, and;
3. Add the salmon fillets to the bowl (the skin side should be up) and marinate for 15 minutes.
4. Spray the air fryer basket with a non-stick cooking spray.
5. Lay the salmon in the basket (skin side down). Turn the air fryer to 400°F (200°C) and allow cooking for 10-12 minutes.
6. Serve the remaining sauce on the side for dipping.

13. Cajun Salmon

Prep Time	5 minutes
Cook Time	10 minutes
Total Time	15 minutes
Servings	2

Ingredients

- 2 teaspoons Cajun seasoning
- 4 oz. skin-on salmon fillets (x2)
- Oil cooking spray
- Salt (optional)

Instructions

1. Use a smooth towel to rinse and dry salmon fillets. Coat fillets with oil spray on both sides.//
2. Add Cajun seasoning mixtures. (The seasoning has salt in it already, this is why salt is not necessary.

3. Place in the air fryer the salmon fillets with the skin-side down.

4. Cook at 360°F (180°C) for 8 to 10 minutes until you are satisfied with the doneness.

Serving Suggestion: Serve with a simple salad.

Nutritional Informational

Calories: 103Cal | Carbohydrates: 0.8g | Fat: 7g| Cholesterol: 24mg| Protein: 10g | Fiber: 2g

14. Asian Salmon

Prep Time	5 minutes
Cook Time	10 minutes
Total Time	15 minutes
Servings	4

Ingredients

- 1 tablespoon brown sugar
- 1 teaspoon Sriracha sauce
- 2 tablespoons soy sauce
- 2 teaspoons cornstarch
- 6 oz. salmon fillets (x4)
- Cooking spray

Instructions

1. In a bowl, whisk the soy sauce, brown sugar, corn starch, and sriracha together.
2. Use a clean towel to rinse and dry salmon fillets. Use the cooking spray to spray the air fryer basket minimally.

3. Place skin-side down salmon fillets in the air fryer basket.
4. Use a pastry brush to generously brush filets with a mixture of soy sauce.
5. Cook at 360°F (180°C) for 8 to 10 minutes in an air fryer until salmon flakes with a fork easily.
6. Brush with more soy sauce mixture halfway through cooking.

Nutritional Informational

Calories: 490Cal | Carbohydrates: 4.6g | Fat: 28g| Cholesterol: 143mg| Protein: 51g | Sugar: 3g

15. Salmon and Cauliflower Rice Bowls

Prep Time	5 minutes
Cook Time	13 minutes
Total Time	18 minutes
Servings	2

Ingredients

- 1 cup arugula
- 1 lemon, halved
- 1 tablespoon olive oil
- 1/2 teaspoon garlic powder
- 2 (6 oz.) salmon fillets
- 2 cups cauliflower rice
- cooking spray
- salt and ground black pepper

Instructions

1. Use a clean towel to rinse and dry salmon fillets. Coat fillets with oil spray generously on both sides.
2. Season with black ground pepper and salt.

3. Place your seasoned salmon in the air fryer basket with the skin-side down

4. Cook at 360°F (182°C) for 8 to 10 minutes, until salmon flakes readily with a fork.

5. Warm olive oil in a medium heated skillet. Add cauliflower rice, garlic powder, salt, and pepper, and cook for about 5-7 minutes, until cauliflower is tender. *ensure to stir continuously.

6. Divide and serve immediately, the cauliflower rice, salmon fillets, arugula, and lemon. *serve them in halves between bowls.

Quick Note:

At most stores, you can buy a riced cauliflower. Alternatively, pulse 3 cups of cauliflower florets in the food processor until the cauliflower is the size of rice grains.

Nutritional Informational

Calories: 572Cal | Carbohydrates: 4.6g | Fat: 10.2g| Cholesterol: 143mg| Protein: 53g | Saturated fat: 5g

16. Salmon & Asparagus

Prep Time	5 minutes
Cook Time	8 minutes
Total Time	13 minutes
Servings	2

Ingredients

- 6 oz. filets fresh Alaskan salmon (deboned) x2
- 2 tablespoons (chopped fresh parsley)
- 2 tablespoons (chopped fresh dill)
- 1 tablespoon olive oil
- 1 bunch asparagus (~500 grams)
- 1 1/2 tablespoons lemon juice
- Salt and pepper, to taste

Instructions

1. Mix the lemon juice, olive oil, dill, parsley, salt, and pepper in a small bowl.

2. Coat the salmon leash with ¾ of the dill and parsley mixture with a spoon.

3. Add the asparagus and the remaining mixture in a medium bowl, and mix well to combine.

4. Add asparagus to the basket of the air fryer, spreading uniformly through the bottom.

5. Place the fillets of salmon on top, so it can rest on the asparagus.

6. Cook at 400°F (200°C) for 6-8 minutes, depending on the thickness of your salmon and your preference.

Nutritional Informational

Calories: 391Cal | Carbohydrates: 9g | Fat: 19g| Cholesterol: 143mg| Protein: 48g | Sugar: 4g |saturated fat: 4g

17. Tandoori Salmon

Course: Dinner; Cuisine: Indian

Prep Time	5 minutes
Cook Time	10 minutes
Total Time	15 minutes
Servings	2

Ingredients

- Olive oil
- 2 teaspoons Tandoori seasoning
- 6 oz. skin-on salmon fillets (1.5 inches thick) x2

Instructions

1. Pat dry the fillets of the salmon. Brush the top with olive oil.

2. Sprinkle over the oiled salmon fillets the Tandoori seasoning— approximately 1 teaspoon per filet. Alternatively, you can combine the Tandoori masala and olive oil first, and spread it through the salmon fillets.

3. Place the fillets of seasoned salmon in the air fryer basket. Turn to 375°F (190°C) and cook for 8-10 minutes.

18. Crumbed Fish

Prep Time	10 minutes
Cook Time	12 minutes
Total Time	22 minutes
Servings	2

Ingredients

- 2 tablespoons vegetable oil
- 2 flounder fillets
- 1/2 lemon (sliced)
- 1/2 egg (beaten)
- 1/2 cup dry bread crumbs

Instructions

1. Preheat your air fryer to 350°F (180°C).
2. In a pan, combine bread crumbs and oil. Stir until the blend becomes crumbly and loose.
3. Dip fillets of fish into the egg; shake off any surplus. Dip the fillets into the mixture of the bread crumb; coat uniformly and completely.

4. In the preheated air fryer, lay the covered fillets gently. Cook for about 12 minutes, until fish flakes readily. Garnish with slices of lemon.

Nutritional Informational

Calories: 350Cal | Carbohydrates: 25.2g | Fat: 17.8g| Cholesterol: 112mg| Protein: 27.2g | Sugar: 2g | saturated fat: 3g | fiber: 2.5g

19. Fish Cake Recipe

Chill Time	30 minutes
Prep Time	15 minutes
Cook Time	15 minutes
Total Time	60 minutes
Servings	6

Ingredients

- 10 oz. mashed potatoes
- 10 oz. fish of your choice
- 1/2 cup Panko bread crumbs.
- 1 tablespoon grainy Dijon mustard
- 1 tablespoon chopped green onion
- 1 egg
- salt and pepper (to taste)
- cooking spray

☞ *Instructions*

A. **To Make the Fish Cakes**:

1. Take about 2 large potatoes or up to 4 medium-sized. Peel, cut and boil until tender. Once cooked, drain and mash (that should be enough to make 10 ounces), then set it aside.

2. Combine the fish, egg, pepper, and salt in a food processor. Pulse the combination up to three until smooth.

3. In a large bowl, combine the mashed potatoes, fish mixture, and green onion.

4. With a rim, place the breadcrumbs in a shallow dish.

5. Divide the fish mixture into 6 portions.

6. Transform each portion into a patty, i.e., roll into a ball-like shape while pressing to form a thick patty. Coat each patty with the breadcrumbs.

7. Place the patties on a plate, cover with plastic wrap and place in the fridge for at least 30 minutes to chill.

B. **To Cook the Fish Cakes**:

1. Adjust your air fryer to 400°F (200°C)

2. Remove the fish cakes from the fridge.

3. Place them in your air fryer's cooking basket. Depending on your model, if they don't all fit in the basket, you may have to cook them in 2 batches.

4. Sprinkle them lightly on both sides with a cooking spray.

5. Cook for 10-15 minutes in the air fryer or until the recipe turns golden brown. Turn the patties over after 5-6 minutes from cooking.

<u>Serving suggestion</u>: Serve with tartar sauce, or even sour cream.

Nutritional Informational

Calories: 240Cal | Carbohydrates: 42g | Fat: 1g| Cholesterol: 32.8mg| Protein: 6g | fiber: 2.5g | Sugar: 2g

20. Grilled Fish Fillet with Pesto Sauce

Prep Time	10 minutes
Cook Time	8 minutes
Total Time	18 minutes
Servings	3

Ingredients

- 1 bunch fresh basil (1/2 oz.)
- 1 cup extra virgin olive oil
- 1 tablespoon grated parmesan cheese
- 1 tablespoon olive oil
- 2 garlic cloves
- 2 tablespoon pine nuts
- 2/5 lb. of white fish fillets (x3)
- Pepper & salt

Instructions

1. Preheat the air fryer to 320° F (160°C).

2. Brush with oil the fish fillets and season with salt and pepper. Place in the air fryer's cooking basket.

3. Set air fryer to 8 minutes of cooking time at the preheated temperature.

4. Combine the basil leaves, pine nuts, parmesan cheese, garlic, olive oil, and position them in a food processor or pestle and mortar. Using the food processor, pulse until it turns into a sauce, and you can grind using pestle and mortar if you wish. Add salt to taste.

5. Place the fillets of fish on a serving plate and serve with pesto sauce.

Tip: you can as well cover the fish in pesto sauce and cover with breadcrumbs before cooking it in the air fryer.

21. Fried Catfish

Course: dinner, lunch

Prep Time	20 minutes
Cook Time	25 minutes
Total Time	45 minutes
Servings	2

Ingredients

- 2 catfish fillets
- 1/2 tablespoon olive oil
- 1/2 tablespoon chopped parsley (optional)
- 1/8 cup seasoned fish fry

Instructions

1. Preheat the air fryer to 400ºF (200ºC).
2. Rinse and pat the catfish dry.
3. In a big Ziploc bag, pour the fish fry seasoning. Add the catfish to the bag. Seal and shake your bag. Ensure that the entire filet is seasoned.

4. On the top of each fillet, spray olive oil lightly.

5. In the Air Fryer basket, place the filet and cook for 10 minutes.

6. Flip over the fish and cook another 10 minutes.

7. Flip over the fish once again and cook for another 2-3 minutes or until desired crispness is achieved.

8. Top with parsley.

Quick Note:

The fillet should be fully coated with the fish fry seasoning but not overly coated, and therefore you are required to use your judgment to determine how much seasoning you will need.

Cooking time will vary based on the fish size and the air fryer brand you are using.

Calories: **208Cal**

VEGETABLE RECIPES FOR YOUR AIR FRYER

- Air Roasted Asparagus
- Buffalo Cauliflower
- Crispy Broccoli
- Avocado Fries
- Sweet Potatoes Fries
- Zucchini Fries
- Artichoke Hearts
- Crispy Eggplants
- Fried Green Tomatoes
- Kale Chips

Etc.

Chapter Seven: Vegetable Recipes for air fryer

Cooking vegetables in the air fryer gives an outcome similar to roasting, but slightly crispier on the outside.

Vegetables come in different texture, but for this course, vegetables will be grouped into two categories: firm and tender for convenience. Vegetables like broccoli, cucumber, bell pepper, zucchini, tomato, squash, asparagus, etc. are regarded as tender veggies. Generally, quick-cooking vegetables are tender.

The firm veggies take longer to cook than the tender veggies, and they are very enjoyable to fry. Examples include carrots, potatoes, beets, butternuts.

What about frozen vegetables?

There is no problem with frozen vegetables. You can cook them in the air fryer as well. All you need to do is to add a few minutes to the recommended cooking time given for the vegetable recipe in the unfrozen form.

Vegetables – air fryer cooking time chart

Vegetables	Temperature (°F)/(°C)	Time (Minutes)
Asparagus	400/200	5
Beets (whole)	400/200	40
Broccoli	400/200	6
Brussels sprouts (halved)	380/190	15
Carrots (sliced 1/2 inch)	380/190	15
Cauliflower (florets)	400/200	12
Corn on the cob	390/200	6
Eggplant (1 1/2 inch cubes)	400/200	15
Green beans	400/200	5

Kale leaves	250/120	12
Mushrooms (sliced 1/4 inch)	400/200	5
Onions (pearl)	400/200	10
Parsnips (1/2 inch chunks)	380/190	15
Peppers (1-inch chunks)	400/200	15
Potatoes (small baby, 1.5 lbs.)	400/200	15
Potatoes (1-inch chunks)	400/200	12
Potatoes (baked whole)	400/200	40
Squash (1/2 inch chunks)	400/200	12
Sweet potato (baked)	380/190	35

Tomatoes (cherry)	400/200	4
Tomatoes (halves)	350/180	10
Zucchini (1/2 inch sticks)	400/200	12

22. Air Roasted Asparagus

Course: Side Dish, Cuisine: Air Fryer

Prep Time	5 minutes
Cook Time	10 minutes
Total Time	15 minutes
Servings	4

Calories: **32Cal**

Ingredients

- 1 lb. fresh asparagus, (with ends trimmed)
- 1-2 teaspoons olive oil
- Black pepper
- Salt, to taste

Instructions

1. Coat the asparagus with olive oil, and season with pepper and salt.

2. Air fry for 8-10 minutes at 380ºF (190ºC), depending on the thickness. Shake and turn asparagus halfway their cooking.

Serving suggestion: Asparagus is a fantastic side dish to accompany any meal.

Cooking tips

Add your favorite dry spices before cooking for extra flavor and taste. Also, adjust cooking time based on the thickness of the asparagus.

Coat the tips of the asparagus with oil to avoid premature burning.

23. Buffalo Cauliflower

Course: Appetizer; Cuisine: Vegan

Prep Time	5 minutes
Cook Time	15 minutes
Total Time	20 minutes
Servings	4

Calories: **200Cal**

Ingredients

Cauliflower

- 4 cups cauliflower florets – each about the size of two baby carrots put side by side.
- 1 cup panko breadcrumbs mixed with;
- 1 teaspoon of sea salt

Buffalo Coating

- 1/4 cup melted vegan butter
- 1/4 cup vegan Buffalo sauce

Dipping

- Vegan mayo

☞ *Instructions*

1. Melt the vegan butter in a mug using your microwave heater, then whisk into the buffalo sauce.

2. Dip each floret in the butter-buffalo mixture, holding by the stem. (A few drops of sauce from the floret is okay).

3. Dredge the dipped floret in the panko/salt mixture, and then place it in the air fryer's basket.

4. Air fry at 350°F (180°C) for 15 minutes, shaking about 2-3 times during this interval. Your cauliflower is done when the florets are a little bit browned.

5. Serve with your dipping sauce of choice.

Quick Notes

Buffalo cauliflower doesn't stay crunchy for too long, so serve and eat immediately for maximum satisfaction.

You also have the option if reheating in the air fryer or oven so they can become crunchy again. Using a microwave to reheat will not give a desirable output.

24. Crispy Broccoli

Prep Time	5 minutes
Cook Time	15 minutes
Total Time	20 minutes
Servings	4

Calories: **105 Cal**

Ingredients

- 1 lb. broccoli, cut into bite-sized pieces
- 1/2 teaspoon garlic powder
- 2 tablespoons oil
- Fresh cracked black pepper, to taste
- Fresh lemon wedges
- Salt, to taste

Instructions

1. To a large bowl, add broccoli and drizzle evenly with olive oil.
2. Season the broccoli with pepper, garlic powder, and salt.

3. Air fry the broccoli at 380°F (190ºC) for 12-15 minutes, flipping and shaking 2-3 times during the cooking interval, or cook until desired crispness is achieved.

Serving suggestion: Serve with lemon wedges.

Quick Note: If the basket feels full at first, don't worry; it will shrink to half its' size.

25. Avocado Fries

Prep Time	10 minutes
Cook Time	10 minutes
Total Time	20 minutes
Servings	2

Ingredients

- 1 ripe avocado (halved, seeded, peeled and cut into 8 slices)
- 1/4 cup all-purpose flour
- 1/2 teaspoon ground black pepper
- 1/4 teaspoon salt
- 1 egg
- 1 teaspoon water
- 1/2 cup panko bread crumbs
- Cooking spray

Instructions

1. Preheat your air fryer to 400°F (200°C).

2. Mix flour, pepper, and salt in a deep bowl. In a second deep bowl, beat the egg and water together. In a third deep bowl, place the panko.

3. Dredge through the flour, an avocado slice, shaking off excess. Dip into the egg and let go of the excess drop off.

4. Press the slice into the panko to cover both sides. Set the rest of the slices on a tray and repeat.

5. Spray the slices of the avocado with cooking spray and arrange it in the air fryer. Also, spray the top side of the slices of avocado.

6. Cook for 5 minutes in the preheated air fryer. Turn the slices of avocado over and cook for about 3-5 more minutes until golden.

Nutrition Information

Calories: 319Cal | Carbohydrates: 39.8g | Fat: 18g| Cholesterol: 82mg| Protein: 9.3g

26. Sweet Potato Fries

Course: Side Dish, Snack; Cuisine: American, Western

Prep Time	10 minutes
Cook Time	14 minutes
Total Time	24 minutes
Servings	4

Ingredients

- 5 oz. sweet potatoes (x2)
- 1 tablespoon olive oil
- 1/4 teaspoon fine sea salt
- Cooking spray

Instructions

1. Peel and slice into 1/4 inch thick fries each sweet potato.
2. Mix the olive oil and salt and carefully coat the sweet potato fries.

3. Preheat air fryer to 360ºF (180ºC) and lightly spray the air fryer basket with cooking spray.

4. Cook in one layer, hence there might be need to cook in batches.

5. 8 minutes for (thin fries), up to 14 minutes (thick fries), flipping the fries halfway through the cooking time.

Cooking Tips

- Cut chips uniformly to achieve an evenly cooked fries.
- Turnover at halfway during cooking, to ensure even cooking.

Nutritional Informational

Calories: 86Cal | Carbohydrates: 13g | Fat: 3g | Protein: 1g | Sugar: 2g | fiber: 1g

27. Zucchini, Yellow Squash, and Carrots

Prep Time	10 minutes
Cook Time	35 minutes
Total Time	45 minutes
Servings	2-4

Ingredients

- 1 lb. yellow squash (root and stem ends trimmed and cut into 3/4 inch half-moons)
- 1 lb. zucchini (root and stem ends trimmed and cut into 3/4 inch half-moons)
- 1 tablespoon tarragon leaves, roughly chopped
- 1 teaspoon kosher salt
- 1/2 lb. carrots (peeled & cut into 1-inch cubes)
- 1/2 teaspoon ground white pepper
- 6 teaspoons olive oil

Instructions

1. Combine the carrot cubes in a small bowl with 2 olive oil teaspoons and toss well to mix.

2. Place the carrots in the air fryer's basket, cook at 400°F (200°C) for 5 minutes.

3. Put the zucchini and yellow squash pieces in a medium-sized bowl while the carrots are cooking in the air fryer.

4. Add the remaining 4 olive oil teaspoons and season with salt and pepper. Toss well to toast vegetables.

5. Once the timer is off, add the carrots, yellow squash, and zucchini together to the air Fryer. Close the draw.

6. Cook at the same temperature, but for 30 minutes. Toss the mixture 2 to 3 times during the cooking time interval to ensure even cooking.

7. Remove from the air fryer the vegetables, and toss with tarragon leaves.

Calories: **400 Cal**

28. Zucchini Fries

Prep Time	10 minutes
Cook Time	20 minutes
Total Time	30 minutes
Servings	3

Ingredients

- 1 medium zucchini
- 1/2 cup bread crumbs
- 1/6 cup parmesan cheese
- 1/8 cup butter
- 1/8 teaspoon seasoning salt

Instructions

1. Cut the entire zucchini into pieces of 4 inches. Then slice the bits of zucchini in half, then again in quarters, making them pieces 1/2 inch wide (the sticks should be about 4 inches long and 1/2 inch wide). Get rid of the seeded center.

2. Combine the crumbs, parmesan cheese, and seasoning salt in a bowl. Melt the butter in another bowl.

3. Dip the pieces of zucchini into the butter that has been melted.

4. Then roll them in the mixture of bread crumb.

5. Add the zucchini fries to the basket of the air fryer, (It shouldn't be too full)

6. Fry at 350°F (180°C) for 20 minutes

Serve warm!

29. Zucchini Chips

Prep Time	10 minutes
Cook Time	12 minutes
Total Time	22 minutes
Servings	6

Ingredients

- 1 cup panko bread crumbs
- 3/4 cup grated Parmesan cheese
- 1 medium zucchini (thinly sliced)
- 1 large egg (beaten)
- Cooking spray

Instructions

1. Preheat your air fryer to 350°F (180°C).
2. Combine panko with parmesan cheese on a plate. In another bowl containing your beaten egg, dip 1 slice of zucchini and press to coat in a panko mixture.

3. Place the zucchini slice on a baking rack while you repeat the process for the remaining slices.

4. Lightly spray zucchini slices with spray.

5. Without overlapping the zucchini slices, place as many of them in the air fryer basket.

6. Cook for 10 minutes, flips the zucchini slices with tongs, and cook for an additional 2 minutes.

Nutritional Informational

Calories: 165Cal | Carbohydrates: 21.1g | Fat: 6g| Cholesterol: 80mg| Protein: 12g

30. Crispy Roasted Brussels Sprouts

Prep Time	10 minutes
Cook Time	15 minutes
Total Time	25 minutes
Servings	4

Ingredients

- 1 lb. Brussels sprouts (ends removed and cut into bite-sized pieces)
- 1 tablespoon balsamic vinegar
- 1 tablespoon olive oil
- Black pepper
- Kosher salt

Instructions

1. Put the Brussels sprout in a big bowl.
2. Drizzle oil and balsamic vinegar evenly over Brussels sprout.
3. Add salt & pepper to taste.

4. Toss the Brussels sprouts completely with the oil and balsamic vinegar.

5. Place the Brussels sprout into the air fryer basket. Air fry at 360°F (180°C) for about 15 minutes and stir gently halfway through cooking to ensure even cooking. Continue to fry the Brussels sprout for the rest of the time or until the Brussels is golden brown and cooked

Calories: **85 Cal**

31. Crispy Kale Chips

Prep Time	2 minutes
Cook Time	5 minutes
Total Time	7 minutes
Servings	1

Ingredients

- 1 bunch kale with stems and ribs removed
- 1/2 tablespoon oil or cooking spray
- Freshly ground pepper
- Salt, (to taste)

Instructions

1. Toss the kale with oil, or spray with cooking oil.
2. Season the kale with salt and pepper. Place in the air fryer basket.
3. Set the air fryer to 400°F (200°C) and cook for 5 minutes. Shake the basket halfway through cooking to ensure even cooking.
4. Serve warm.

32. Fried Green Tomatoes

Course: Appetizer; Cuisine: American

Prep Time	5 minutes
Cook Time	12 minutes
Total Time	17 minutes
Servings	2

Ingredients

- 2 large green tomatoes sliced 1/4 inch thick in rounds
- ½ lb. cornmeal
- ½ lb. gluten-free panko
- 2 eggs (beaten)
- Spray oil

Instructions

1. Slice the tomatoes, and put them on a tray.
2. Season with salt and pepper.
3. Beat the eggs and place them in a deep bowl.

4. Mix the panko and cornmeal in a bowl.

5. Dredge the tomato slices slowly through the mixture of the eggs and position them in the panko mixture. Press the panko mixture gently on the tomato slices on all sides.

6. Spray the air fryer basket with the cooking spray. Place up to 3-4 slices of tomato in the basket, depending on the capacity of your air fryer. Spray the top as well.

7. Air fry at 400°F (204°C) for 8 minutes, and flip the slices over, spray the sauce again and cook for extra 4 minutes.

Nutritional Informational

Calories: 504 Cal | Carbohydrates: 88g | Fat: 12g| Cholesterol: 181mg| Protein: 12g | Sugar: 1g | saturated fat: 3g | fiber: 7g

33. Honey Roasted Carrots

Prep Time	5 minutes
Cook Time	12 minutes
Total Time	17 minutes
Servings	2

Ingredients

- 1 tablespoon of honey
- 1 tablespoon of Extra virgin olive oil (EVOO)
- 3 cups of baby carrots
- Dill
- Salt and pepper to taste

Instructions

1. In a large mixing bowl, add and coat the carrots with olive oil, honey, pepper, and salt.
2. Place your mixture in the air fryer, then set the temperature to 390°F (200°C), for 12 minutes.
3. Remove from the air fryer, sprinkle some dill on them, and serve.

34. Crispy Eggplant Parmesan

Course: Dinner, Lunch, Main Course; Cuisine: American

Prep Time	20 minutes
Cook Time	12 minutes
Total Time	32 minutes
Servings	4

Ingredients

- 2/3 cup grated mozzarella cheese
- 2/3 cup marinara sauce
- 1 egg beaten
- 1 large eggplant (cut into ½ inch thick slices)
- 1/2 cup gluten-free breadcrumbs or regular breadcrumbs
- 2 tablespoon grated parmesan cheese

Instructions

1. Preheat the air fryer to 250°F (120°C).
2. Season the eggplant slices with salt, and leave to stand for 20 minutes and pat dry.

3. In a deep bowl, mix the breadcrumbs with the parmesan cheese. Beat the egg in another bowl.
4. Dip each eggplant slices in the beaten egg, until excess egg drip off.
5. Dip the eggplant slices in the breadcrumb mixture, coat evenly and set aside.
6. Spray the air fryer basket with oil, add the breaded eggplant slices.
7. Cook for 6-9 minutes, or until you achieve a tender texture.
8. Top the breaded eggplant slices with marinara sauce and mozzarella cheese.
9. Cook for an additional 2 minutes until cheese is melted on the breaded eggplant.
10. Remove your eggplant parmesan from the air fryer and serve.

Nutritional Informational

Calories: 167Cal | Carbohydrates: 19g | Fat: 7.2g| Cholesterol: 57mg| Protein: 9g | Sugar: 6g | saturated fat: 3g | fiber: 4g

35. Artichoke Hearts

Prep Time	10 minutes
Cook Time	15 minutes
Total Time	25 minutes
Servings	4

Ingredients

- 1 cup panko breadcrumbs
- 1/3 cup grated Parmesan
- Salt, to taste
- Pepper to taste
- Parsley
- 1/2 cup mayonnaise
- 2-3 cans Reese Quartered Artichokes (drained & dried)

Instructions

1. Drain artichokes in a colander.
2. Mix mayonnaise, salt & pepper in a small bowl, and toss gently.

3. Place the Panko in a zip-top bag, as well as the coated artichokes, and shake well until evenly coated.

4. Place coated artichokes into the air fryer & cook at 400°F (200°C) for 10-15 minutes.

5. Sprinkle with parmesan cheese & parsley and serve.

36. Shishito Peppers with Lime

Course: Appetizer, Side Dish, Snack; Cuisine: Japanese

Prep Time	2 minutes
Cook Time	8 minutes
Total Time	10 minutes
Servings	4

Ingredients

- 1 lemon, cut into wedges
- 1/4 teaspoon kosher salt
- 8 oz. shishito peppers
- Extra virgin olive oil spray (EVOO)

Instructions

1. Preheat the air fryer at 400°F (200°C) for at least 3 minutes.

2. Spray the shishito peppers with the olive oil.

3. Transfer the sprayed shishito peppers into the air fryer and cook at 400°F (200°C) for 8 minutes. Shake the basket

halfway through the cooking time, until soft and slightly blistered.

4. Sprinkle with salt and squeeze with lemon wedges, serve warm.

Chapter Eight: Poultry Recipes for Air Fryer

EASY POULTRY RECIPES FOR AIR FRYER

- Chicken Wings 'n' Sauce
- Panko Breaded Chicken Parmesan with Marinara Sauce
- Turkey Breast Recipe with Lemon Pepper
- Chicken Fajita Dinner
- Buttermilk Fried Chicken
- Satay Chicken Skewers
- Buffalo Chicken Meatballs
- Honey Mustard Chicken Breasts
- Honey Garlic Chicken Wings
- Turkey Breast

37. Chicken Wings 'n' Sauce

Prep Time	5 minutes
Cook Time	30 minutes
Total Time	35 minutes
Servings	4

Ingredients

- 1/4 teaspoon cayenne pepper
- 1/2 cup butter
- 2/3 cup cayenne pepper sauce
- 1 tablespoon olive oil
- 1 teaspoon garlic powder
- 2 tablespoons vinegar
- 2 ½ pounds chicken wings

Instructions

1. Preheat your air fryer to 360°F (180°C).
2. In a big bowl, place the wings. Drizzle oil over the wings until the chicken is uniformly covered.

3. Place half of the wings in the basket of the air fryer and cook for 25 minutes at the same temperature.

4. Use hand cooking tongs to turn wings and allow cooking for another 5 minutes. Transfer the cooked wings to a big bowl. Repeat the same for the wings left to be prepared.

5. In a small saucepan, mix the butter, vinegar, garlic powder, cayenne pepper, pepper sauce, and place over a medium heat source. Stir and warm while you wait for the remaining wings to be cooked.

6. Pour the sauce over the cooked wings and toss to coat evenly.

Nutritional Informational

Calories: 475Cal | Carbohydrates: 7.3g | Sugar: 2g | Fat: 41.5g

38. Panko Breaded Chicken Parmesan with Marinara Sauce

Course dinner, lunch; Cuisine American, Italian

Prep Time	10 minutes
Cook Time	20 minutes
Total Time	30 minutes
Servings	4

Ingredients

- 1 cup panko bread crumbs
- 1/2 cup mozzarella cheese (shredded)
- 1/2 cup parmesan cheese (grated)
- 1/8 cup egg whites
- 16 oz. skinless chicken breast
- 2 teaspoon Italian Seasoning
- 3/4 cup Marinara Sauce
- Cooking spray
- Salt and pepper to taste

Instructions

1. Spray the basket with cooking spray and preheat the air fryer to 400°F (200°C).

2. Horizontally slice the chicken breasts in half, to generate 4 thinner breasts of chicken. Place the chicken breasts on a flat surface and pound to flatten them completely.

3. Grate the parmesan cheese.

4. In a large bowl, dip the chicken breasts, combine and mix the panko breadcrumbs, cheese, and seasonings.

5. Place the egg whites in a sufficiently big bowl. Dip the chicken in the egg whites and then the combination of the breadcrumbs.

6. Place the prepared ingredients in the air fryer. Spray cooking spray on the top of the chicken.

7. At the preheated temperature, cook for seven minutes. Use marinara sauce and shredded mozzarella to top each of the breasts. Cook for another 3 minutes until cheese has melted.

Nutritional Informational

Calories: 332 Cal | Carbohydrates: 13g | Protein: 37g | Fat: 12g

39. Turkey Breast Recipe with Lemon Pepper

Prep Time	5 minutes
Cook Time	55 minutes
Total Time	60 minutes
Servings	6

Ingredients

- 3 lbs. de-boned uncooked turkey breast (or 4 lbs. boned)
- 2 tablespoons oil
- 1 tablespoon Worcestershire sauce
- 1 teaspoon lemon pepper
- 1/2 teaspoon salt, to taste

Instructions

1. Pat the dry turkey.
2. Combine in a bowl, Worcestershire sauce, oil, lemon pepper, and salt.

3. Add the turkey to the marinade, and ensure that the marinade coats the turkey breast completely. Marinate for an hour or two if possible.

4. Oil the air fryer basket lightly. Remove the turkey from the marinade and position the skin side of the turkey breast down in the basket of the air fryer.

5. Air fry at 350°F (180°C) for 25 minutes. Flip the turkey breast to the skin side up, and air fry for another 30-35 minutes. Bone-in turkey breast might require an additional 5-10 minutes of cooking time.

6. This is where a food thermometer is essential. You will have to confirm if the turkey is well cooked by assessing the turkey's internal temperature in the thickest part. If it reads up to 170°F (80°C), then it's okay.

Quick Note

In order to prevent the turkey breast from drying out, particularly if it is skinless, spray the turkey top and edges a few times during cooking with a little oil to maintain it moist.

Some turkey breasts are smaller or sometimes broken into several parts. If you are cooking smaller parts separately, then it takes less time to cook.

Calories: 400 Cal

40. Chicken Fajita Dinner

Prep Time	10 minutes
Cook Time	20 minutes
Total Time	30 minutes
Servings	4

Ingredients

- 1 teaspoon cumin
- 1 teaspoon. salt
- 1 lb. boneless, skinless chicken breast(sliced)
- 1 onion(sliced)
- 1 pinch cayenne
- 1/2 teaspoon black pepper
- 2 teaspoon chili powder
- 2 teaspoon olive oil
- 2 bell peppers (sliced)

Instructions

1. Combine in a bowl the sliced chicken and vegetables.

2. Add olive oil, chili powder, cumin, salt, cayenne, and pepper. Combine and pour the contents into the tray basket of the air fryer.

3. Slide the tray into the air fryer and cook at 360ºF (180ºC) for 17-20 minutes, checking and turning halfway through cooking (around 8-10 minutes time mark).

Serving suggestions

Once the fajitas have finished cooking, serve in tortillas, rice, or a salad with any toppings of your choice.

41. Buttermilk Fried Chicken

Prep Time	5 minutes
Cook Time	30 minutes
Total Time	35 minutes
Servings	4

Ingredients

- 1 lb. boneless, skinless chicken thighs
- 2 teaspoons seasoned salt
- 1 teaspoon ground black pepper
- 1-1/3 cups buttermilk
- 2/3 cup all-purpose flour
- 2/3 cup panko bread crumbs
- 5/8 serving cooking spray

Instructions

1. Place the chicken thighs in a shallow dish. Pour buttermilk over chicken and cool for at least 4hours or preferably overnight.

2. Preheat the air fryer to 380°F (190°C).

3. In a big gallon-sized resealable bag, combine flour, seasoned salt, and pepper.

4. Dredge the chicken thighs in seasoned flour. Dip into the buttermilk once again, and then cover with crumbs of panko bread.

5. Spray nonstick cooking spray on the air fryer basket. Arrange in the basket 1/2 of the chicken thighs to ensure that they aren't touching. Spray cooking spray on the top of each chicken thigh.

6. Cook for 15 minutes in the preheated air fryer. Flip and spray chicken top once again.

7. Continue cooking for 10 minutes or more, until the center is no longer pinky.

8. Use a food thermometer to check the internal temperature of the chicken. The temperature at the center should not be less 165°F, which infers the chicken is well cooked.

Nutritional Informational

Calories: 320Cal | Carbohydrates: 31g | Fat: 12g| Cholesterol: 75mg| Protein: 22.0g

42. Satay Chicken Skewers

Prep Time	10 minutes
Cook Time	10 minutes
Total Time	20 minutes
Servings	4

Ingredients

- 1 lb. boneless chicken tenders
- 1/2 cup soy sauce
- 1/2 cup pineapple juice
- 1/4 cup sesame seed oil
- 4 garlic cloves (chopped)
- 4 scallions (chopped)
- 1 tablespoon freshly grated ginger
- 2 teaspoons toasted sesame seeds
- Black pepper

Instructions

1. Skewer on wooden skewer each piece of chicken tender.
2. Mix all the other ingredients in a big bowl.

3. Add the skewed chicken to the bowl and ensure that the mix covers them completely.

4. Cover the bowl and cool for 4 hours or overnight.

5. Preheat air fryer to 390°F (200°C).

6. Pat dry the chicken with a paper towel.

7. Lay the skewers in the air fryer and cook for 7-10 minutes, depending on how you want it to be. Don't overcrowd the basket.

8. Serve!

43. Buffalo Chicken Meatballs

Prep Time	5 minutes
Cook Time	15 minutes
Total Time	20 minutes
Servings	5

Ingredients

- 1lb. ground chicken
- 1 large egg
- 1 teaspoon garlic powder
- 1/2 cup breadcrumbs
- 1/2 cup buffalo sauce – (2 portions)
- 1/2 teaspoon onion powder
- 1/2 teaspoon salt

Instructions

1. Mix the breadcrumbs, buffalo sauce (1st portion), ground chicken, garlic powder, onion powder, and salt.

2. Spray the air fryer basket.

3. Roll meat in 8-10 meatballs of golf-ball size. Put the meatballs in the basket of the air fryer (Depending on the air fryer size).

4. Air fry for 12 minutes at 400°F (200°C). At 12 minutes, check for doneness. Depending on meatballs and air fryer size, you might have to extend the cooking time by another 3-5 minutes.

5. Toss the meatballs with the rest of the sauce (second portion).

Serving Suggestion

Serve with blue cheese dip, celery and carrots.

Nutritional Informational

Calories: 231Cal | Carbohydrates: 11g | Fat: 14g| Cholesterol: 120mg| Protein: 27g | Sugar: 1g | saturated fat: 3g | fiber: 1g

44. Honey Mustard Chicken Breasts

Prep Time	10 minutes
Cook Time	20 minutes
Total Time	30 minutes
Servings	6

Ingredients

- ¼ teaspoon ground black pepper
- ¾ teaspoon salt
- 2 tablespoons minced fresh rosemary
- 3 tablespoons honey
- 6 oz. boneless skinless chicken breasts (x6)
- 6 tablespoons Dijon mustard
- Cooking spray

Instructions

1. Preheat the air fryer to 350°F (180°C).
2. Stir in a small bowl the honey, Dijon mustard, fresh rosemary, salt, and pepper.
3. Rub mustard mixture all through the entire chicken breast.

4. Spray the air fryer basket with cooking spray. Put the chicken breasts in the basket of the air fryer.

5. Cook chicken breasts in the air fryer at 350°F (180°C), and cook for 20minutes or more, until the cooked chicken breast attains an internal temperature of 165 °F (74°C).

Nutritional Informational

Calories: 245Cal | Carbohydrates: 11g | Fat: 6g| Cholesterol: 102mg| Protein: 38g | saturated fat: 3g

45. Honey Garlic Chicken Wings

Course: Appetizer, Lunch Dinner; Cuisine: American

Prep Time	10 minutes
Cook Time	35 minutes
Total Time	45 minutes
Servings	2

Ingredients

- 16 pieces of chicken wings
- 4 tablespoons fresh garlic minced
- 1/2 teaspoon kosher salt
- 1/4 cup clover honey
- 1/4 cup butter
- 1/8 cup fresh water (or more as needed)
- 3/4 cup potato starch

Instructions

1. Pat and dry chicken wings with a paper towel
2. Add potato starch to a bowl and coat chicken wings with it.
3. Place the coated chicken wings into the air fryer

4. Cook for 25 minutes at 380ºF (193ºC), shaking the basket about 3-4 times during the cooking time.

5. If you desire very dry and crispy chicken wings, you can cook at 400ºF (204ºC) for another 7-10 minutes.

6. In a small saucepan, melt butter on low heat, and sauté the garlic for 4 minutes.

7. Add honey and salt and boil gently on a low heat for about 15- 20 minutes, stirring every minute, to prevent the sauce from burning. Add a few drops of water halfway to prevent the sauce from hardening.

8. Remove chicken wings from the air fryer and pour the sauce over it.

Quick Note:

Extra-large wings require more minutes of cooking time than given above. Add a couple of minutes to the recommended time, but maintaining the temperature.

46. Turkey Breast

Course: turkey; Cuisine: American

Prep Time	5 minutes
Cook Time	55 minutes
Total Time	60 minutes
Servings	2

Ingredients

- 1 tablespoon olive oil
- 2 teaspoons kosher salt
- 4-pound turkey breast on the bone with skin (ribs removed)
- 2 tablespoon butter *
- 1 teaspoon dried thyme *
- 1/2 teaspoon paprika *
- 1/2 teaspoon dried oregano *

Instructions

1. Preheat the air fryer to 350°F (180°C)

2. Combine and mix the butter rub ingredients (the ingredients with the * sign) in a small bowl, and gently spread it under the turkey breast skin.

3. Use 1/2 Tbsp. of oil to rub the entire surface of the turkey breast, season with salt, and seasoning. Add the other 1/2 Tbsp. oil entirely on the skin side of the turkey. Place in the air fryer.

4. Cook skin down for 20 minutes, flip and cook for another 30 minutes or more. Just ensure you cook until the internal temperature of the turkey using an instant-read food thermometer is 165°F (74°C).

5. Allow the turkey to settle for about 10-15 minutes, before proceeding to carve it.

Quick Note

Depending on the size of the breast, cooking time might vary slightly from what is given above.

Chapter Nine: Sweets Recipes

SWEETS RECIPES FOR YOUR AIR FRYER

Churros with Chocolate Sauce

Doughnuts

Baked Banana Bread

Cinnamon Apple

Pineapple Cake

Cinnamon Toast

47. Churros with Chocolate Sauce

Active Time	30 minutes
Total Time	90 minutes
Servings	4

Ingredients

- 4 large eggs
- 4 teaspoons ground cinnamon
- 8 oz. bittersweet baking chocolate (finely chopped)
- 6 tablespoons heavy cream
- 4 tablespoons vanilla kefir
- 1 cup of water
- 2/3 cup granulated sugar
- 1/2 teaspoon kosher salt
- 1/2 cup +4 tbsp. unsalted butter (divided into 2 portions)
- 1 cup all-purpose flour

Instructions

Phase 1 (Preparing your churros)

1. In a small saucepan over a medium heated source, place 1/2 cup of the butter, then water and salt. After about 30-45 seconds, reduce the heat from medium to low.

2. Add flour, and stir vigorously with a wooden spoon or spatula, continue until dough is smooth. You should accomplish this in less than 60 seconds.

3. While cooking, stir continuously until dough begins to pull off the sides of the pan. This should occur within 2-3 minutes.

4. Transfer dough into a large bowl and stir continuously until it is partially cooled, allow about 2-3 minutes for this.

5. Add egg the first egg; stir until completely smooth, then add the second and do the same. Repeat for the third and fourth.

6. Now, transfer mixture to a piping bag fitted with a medium star tip. Refrigerate for about 30 minutes.

Phase 2 (Air frying your churros)

1. After chilling, place the pipes in a single layer into the air fryer basket, and cook at 380°F (190°C) for 10 minutes, or until golden. (The number of pipes depends on the inches of the pipes and the size of your air fryer).

2. In a medium bowl, stir the sugar and cinnamon.

3. Use the 4 tbsp. melted butter, to brush the cooked churros and roll in into sugar mixture to coat.

Phase 3 (Chocolate Sauce)

1. Using a small bowl (microwave- friendly), place chocolate and cream and microwave on high for about 30-45 seconds. Remove when it is melted and smooth. (Remember to stir at least once halfway into the microwaving).

2. Stir in kefir.

Your churros are ready to be served with the chocolate sauce.

Nutritional Informational

Calories: 177Cal | Carbohydrates: 15.6g | Fat: 12g| Cholesterol: 132mg| Protein: 5g | Sugar: 7g | Saturated fat: 7g | Fiber: 1g

48. Doughnuts

Active Time	40 minutes
Total Time	2 hrs. 10 minutes
Servings	8

Ingredients

- 1 cup powdered sugar
- 1 large egg (beaten)
- 1 teaspoon active dry yeast
- 1/4 cup warm water, warmed (~110°F)
- 1/4 cup whole milk, at room temperature
- 1/4 cup + 1/2 teaspoon. granulated sugar (divided into two portions)
- 1/4 teaspoon kosher salt
- 2 cups all-purpose flour
- 2 tablespoons unsalted butter (melted)
- 4 teaspoons tap water

☞ *Instructions*

Phase 1

1. In a small bowl, stir yeast, half tsp. granulated sugar in water. Let it stand for about 5 minutes until it turns foamy.

2. Mix the flour, the 1/4 cup granulated sugar left, and salt in a medium bowl. Add butter, milk, yeast mixture, and egg. Stir with a wooden spatula or spoon until a soft dough is formed.

3. Turn dough onto a surface and knead until smooth. Transfer dough into a lightly oiled bowl and cover for about 60 minutes, to allow dough rise to about twice the initial size.

Phase 2

1. Turn dough onto a moderately floured surface, and gently roll dough into 1/4- inch thickness.

2. Using a 3-inch round cutter, cut out 8 doughnuts, and remove the center of the doughnuts using a 1-inch round cutter.

3. Cover the doughnuts with plastic wrap, and allow to stand for about 30 minutes, when it must have risen again.

Phase 3

1. Depending on the size of the air fryer, place in a single layer 4 doughnuts or more (2 holes and 2 non-hole).

2. Cook for 5 minutes at 360°F (180°C).

Phase 4

1. In a medium bowl, whisk the powdered sugar with the tap water until smooth to form a glaze.

2. Dip the doughnuts in the glaze, and place on a wire rack set over a rimmed baking sheet, so that excess glaze can drip-off. Allow glaze to stand and harden. After 10 minutes, your snacks are ready.

Nutritional Informational

Calories: 230Cal | Carbohydrates: 42g | Fat: 5g|Saturated fat: 2g| Unsaturated fat: 1g |Protein: 5g | Sugar: 22g | Added sugar: 20g| Fiber: 1g

49. Baked Banana Bread

Prep Time	10 minutes
Cook Time	25 minutes
Total Time	35 minutes
Servings	2

Ingredients

- 1 lb. self-rising flour
- 1/2 teaspoon bicarbonate Soda
- 5 oz. butter
- 2/3 lb. caster sugar
- 4 medium eggs
- 2lbs. bananas weight with peeling
- 7 oz. chopped walnuts

Instructions

1. Preheat the air fryer to 360ºF (180ºC)
2. Mix the flour with bicarbonate soda

3. In another bowl, mix the butter and the sugar until pale and fluffy, add the eggs one after the other. Pour and mix with the flour, adding walnuts.

4. Peel the bananas, mash them up, and add to your flour mixture.

5. Put the mixture into a greased tin can, slot into your air fryer, and cook for 10 minutes at the preheated temperature. Continue cooking, and this time reduce the temperature to (350°F) 170°C for 15 minutes.

Ready to Serve!

Quick Notes

If you are not cool with walnut, you might choose not to add it. You can add extra flavors.

Nutritional Informational

Calories: 3120Cal | Carbohydrates: 430g | Fat: 122g | Saturated fat: 46g | Protein: 60g | Sugar: 222g | Fiber: 20g | Cholesterol: 480mg

50. Cinnamon Apple Chips with Almond Yogurt Dip

Active Time	10 minutes
Total Time	25 minutes
Servings	4

Ingredients

- 1 apple about 8 oz. size (Fuji)
- 1 tablespoon almond butter
- 1 teaspoon ground cinnamon
- 1 teaspoon honey
- 1/4 cup plain low-fat Greek yogurt
- 2 teaspoons canola oil
- Cooking spray

Instructions

1. On a mandoline slicer, thinly slice the apple.
2. Place the apple slices in a bowl, toss to coat evenly with oil and cinnamon.
3. Spray the air fryer basket with the cooking spray.

4. On a single layer, place about 6-8 slices of apple in the air fryer basket. Cook the apple slices for 10-12 minutes at 360ºF (180ºC), while flipping the slices every 3 minutes to flatten them.

5. Stir yogurt, almond butter, and honey in a bowl until smooth.

6. Serve the cooked apple slices with the dipping sauce.

Tip: you can use honeycrisp apple as an alternative to Fuji.

Nutritional Informational

Calories: 110Cal | Carbohydrates: 18g | Fat: 3g|Saturated fat: 1g| Unsaturated fat: 2g |Protein: 1g | Sugar: 5g| Fiber: 3g|

51. Apple Dumplings

Prep Time	25 minutes
Cook Time	35 minutes
Total Time	60 minutes
Servings	4

Ingredients

- 4 small apples
- 2 tablespoon brown sugar
- 4 sheets puff pastry
- 4 tablespoons butter (melted)
- 4 tablespoons raisins

Instructions

1. Preheat your air fryer to 350°F (180°C)
2. Core and peel the apples.
3. In a bowl, mix the brown sugar with the raisins. Put the four apples on a puff pastry sheet each, and fill the

core with the raisins and sugar mixture. Fold the pastry around the apple.

4. Brush the dough with the melted butter.

5. Place in the preheated air fryer, and allow baking for 20-25 minutes, or until golden brown. Flip over during the cooking interval to ensure uniform cooking.

6. Allow to cool, and serve.

Quick Tip

Raisins can be replaced with sultanas.

Serving suggestion: Serve with ice cream.

52. Pineapple Cake

Prep Time	10 minutes
Cook Time	40 minutes
Total Time	50 minutes
Servings	8

Ingredients

- 1 lb. self-raising Flour
- 140 oz. pineapple chopped into chunks
- 200 ml Pineapple Juice
- 40 oz. dark chocolate grated
- 2 medium egg
- 4 tablespoon whole Milk
- 2/5 lb. butter
- 2/5 lb. caster sugar

Instructions

1. Preheat the air fryer to 392ºF (200ºC)

2. Mix the butter with the flour in a large bowl, until it looks like breadcrumbs.
3. Add the sugar, and stir, add the pineapple chunks as well as the juice and add the dark chocolate. Set aside.
4. Beat the egg and mix it with milk in another bowl.
5. Add and mix all liquid to the flour-butter mixture, to form a soft cake mixture.
6. Oil the cake-can before placing in the air fryer, and cook for 40 minutes at the preheated temperature.
7. Allow to rest for few minutes and then serve.

Nutritional Informational

Calories: 600Cal | Carbohydrates: 80g | Fat: 27g|Saturated fat: 15g |Protein: 10g | Sugar: 30g| Fiber: 3g|Cholesterol: 97mg

53. Cinnamon Toast

Course: Breakfast

Prep Time	5 minutes
Cook Time	5 minutes
Total Time	10 minutes
Servings	4

Ingredients

- 1 1/2 teaspoons ground cinnamon
- 1 1/2 teaspoons pure vanilla extract (you can use your desirable flavor as well)
- 1 pinch kosher salt
- 1 stick butter
- 1/2 cup white sugar
- 12 slices bread (whole wheat)
- 2 pinches freshly ground black pepper *

Instructions

1. Combine your softened mashed butter with cinnamon, sugar, vanilla, and salt. Pepper is optional, but if you wish

to use it, you can add it at this stage as well. Stir thoroughly.

2. Spread the mixture onto bread; ensure that it entirely covers the surface.

3. Place slices into the air fryer, as many as your air fryer can take.

4. Set your air fryer at 400°F (200°C) and cook for 5 minutes.

5. Remove from the air fryer and cut it diagonally.

6. Serve immediately.

Nutritional Informational

Calories: 352Cal | Carbohydrates: 40g | Fat: 15g | Saturated fat: 10g | Protein: 10g | Sugar: 20g | Fiber: 3g | Cholesterol: 40mg

Chapter Ten: Beef, Pork and Mushroom Recipes

BEEF, PORK AND MUSHROOM RECIPES FOR YOUR AIR FRYER

Fried Steak

Pork Loin

Beef and Broccoli

Garlic Mushroom

Pork Chop

Breaded Mushroom

54. Fried Steak

Prep Time	5 minutes
Cook Time	25 minutes
Total Time	30 minutes
Servings	4

Ingredients

- 2 teaspoon olive oil
- 1 teaspoon garlic powder (optional)
- 4 (6 oz.) steaks, 3/4" thick (rinsed and patted dry)
- Butter
- Pepper, to taste
- Salt, to taste

Instructions

1. Preheat the air fryer for 5 minutes at 400°F (200°C)
2. Coat the steaks with olive oil lightly
3. Season the steaks with salt and pepper, and with garlic powder (optional)

4. Air fry at 400°F (200°C) for 15-25 minutes, flip the steaks at halfway of cook time. (The cook time is a function of the thickness of the steaks).

5. Pat the top of the steak with butter, cover with foil, and allow it to rest for 5 minutes.

6. Serve.

55. Pork Loin

Course Main Course; Cuisine: American

Prep Time	5 minutes
Cook Time	20 minutes
Total Time	25 minutes
Servings	4

Ingredients

- 1 lb. pork tenderloin
- 2 tablespoon garlic scape pesto
- Non-stick cooking spray
- Salt
- Pepper

Instructions

1. Pat tenderloin dry. Coat all sides with non-stick cooking spray.
2. Season both sides with salt, pepper and garlic scape
3. Spray the tray and rack of the air fryer with cooking spray.

4. Cook one side at 400°F (200°C) for 10 minutes. Carefully remove from the air fryer and flip over to the other side and cook at the same time interval.

5. Use your food thermometer to check if the internal temperature of the meat is up to 140°F, but not more than 165°F.

56. Beef and Broccoli

Course: Main Course, Cuisine: Chinese

Prep Time	60 minutes
Cook Time	20 minutes
Total Time	80 minutes
Servings	3

Ingredients

- 1 lb. broccoli florets
- 1 teaspoon minced garlic
- 1 teaspoon minced ginger
- 1/2 lb. round steak
- 1/3 cup oyster sauce
- 2 tablespoon sesame oil
- 2 tablespoon soy sauce

Instructions

1. In a medium bowl, mix all the ingredients and allow them to marinate for 50-60 minutes.

2. Cook at 350°F for 15 minutes. Shake 2-3 times during the cooking interval.

57. Garlic Mushrooms

Course: Side dish

Prep Time	10 minutes
Cook Time	15 minutes
Total Time	25 minutes
Servings	4

Ingredients

- 16 oz. mushrooms (washed and dried)
- 2 tablespoon chopped parsley
- 2 teaspoon soy sauce
- 1 teaspoon garlic powder
- 4 tablespoons olive oil
- Black pepper (to taste)
- Kosher salt (to taste)

Instructions

1. Cut mushrooms into the desired size, (half or quarters recommended).

2. In a bowl, add the cut mushrooms and toss with oil, soy sauce, garlic powder, pepper, and salt.

3. Place the mixture in the air fryer, air fry for 12-15 minutes at 380ºF (190ºC). Shake halfway through the cooking time.

4. Top with chopped parsley and serve.

58. Pork Chop

Prep Time	5 minutes
Cook Time	15 minutes
Total Time	20 minutes
Servings	4

Ingredients

- 4 boneless pork chops
- 1 teaspoon garlic powder
- 1 teaspoon kosher salt
- 1 teaspoon onion powder
- 1 teaspoon paprika
- 1/2 cup freshly grated parmesan
- 1/2 teaspoon freshly ground black pepper
- 2 tablespoon extra-virgin olive oil (EVOO)

Instructions

1. Using paper towels, pat pork dry, coat with oil.
2. Mix parmesan and all other ingredients (spices) together, coat all sides of the pork with the resulting mixture.
3. Place the pork chops in the basket of the air fryer, set the fryer at 375°F (190°C) for 10 minutes.

59. Breaded Mushrooms

Side dish or appetizer

Prep Time	5 minutes
Cook Time	10 minutes
Total Time	15 minutes
Servings	4

Ingredients

- 1/2 lb. Button mushrooms
- Flour
- 1 egg
- Breadcrumbs
- 3 oz. finely grated Parmigiano Reggiano cheese
- Salt and pepper

Instructions

1. Clean and pat the mushrooms dry with paper towels.
2. Mix the breadcrumbs with the cheese and set aside in a bowl, in another bowl, beat the egg and set aside.

3. Dredge the mushrooms in the flour, then into the egg, and then dip in the breadcrumbs-cheese mix.

4. Place in the air fryer and cook at 180ºF (82ºC) for 8-10 minutes. Shake twice or thrice within the cooking time.

Serving suggestion: Serve warm with your favorite dipping sauce.

About The Author

Anita George, popularly referred to as Annie Dish, is a Food Scientist and a diet coach on several online platforms and blogs. She developed a passion for cooking as early as age 5, and since then she has grown into a professional and pragmatic chef, who experiments several food ingredients against each other, aiming at producing healthy meals.

Being fully aware of the risk that most edible foods pose on human health, she is keen on *healthy-eating*. She is looking forward to helping the world develop more sustainable and healthy approaches to preparing healthy food recipes that pose no harm or significant detrimental health effects. She is working earnestly with her research team, and they looking to breaking new grounds with respect to this.

Appendix A

I. Volumetric Equivalent Table (Liquid)

Approximate values of some larger units are stated below:

Customary quantity	Metric equivalent
1 teaspoon	5 mL
1 tablespoon= 3 teaspoons	15 mL
1 fl. oz.= 2 tablespoons	30 mL
2 fl. oz.= 1/4 cup	60 mL
1/3 cup	80 mL
1 cup=8 fl. oz.= 1/2 pint	240 mL
2 cups=1 pint = 16 fl. oz.	475 mL
4 cups = 1 quart= 32 fl. oz.	950 mL
4 quarts *or* 1 gallon= 128 fl. oz.	3.8 L

1 cup = 250 mL
1 pint = 500 mL
1 quart = 1 L
1 gallon = 4 L

II. Weight conversion table for your recipes

Customary quantity	Metric equivalent
1 ounce	28 g
4 ounces= 1/4 pound	113 g
1/3 pound	150 g
8 ounces=1/2 pound	230 g
2/3 pound	300 g
12 ounces=3/4 pound	340 g
1 pound=16 ounce	450 g

Pls. Note: Fluid ounce (fl. oz.) is different from ounce (oz.). Also, note that approximate values can be used for the above conversion. For instance, 1 oz. =28g from the table, but can be approximated to the nearest ten, which is 30g.

III. Length conversion

Customary quantity	Metric equivalent
1/8 inch	3 mm
1/4 inch	6 mm
1/2 inch	13 mm
3/4 inch	19 mm
1 inch	2.5 cm

Note: 1 cm = 10 mm

Appendix B

Dirty Dozen/ Clean Fifteen

Dirty Dozen	Clean Fifteen
1. Strawberries	1. Avocadoes
2. Spinach	2. Sweet Corn
3. Kale	3. Pineapples
4. Nectarines	4. Sweet Peas Frozen
5. Apples	5. Onions
6. Grapes	6. papayas
7. Peaches	7. Eggplants
8. Cherries	8. Asparagus
9. Pears	9. Kiwis
10. Tomatoes	10. Cabbages
11. Celery	11. Cauliflower
12. Potatoes	12. Cantaloupes
	13. Broccoli
	14. Mushrooms
	15. Honeydew

Appendix C

Air Fryer Conversion Chart

I. Fast Food

	Temperature	Time(Minutes)
Burgers	360°F/180°C	15
Chicken Nuggets	360°F/180°C	10
Chicken Dippers	360°F/180°C	15
Fish and Chips	360°F/180°C	15
Mozzarella Sticks	360°F/180°C	5
Onion Rings	360°F/180°C	8
Pizza	360°F/180°C	10

II. Sweet Recipes Frying

	Temperature	Time(Minutes)
Apple Chips	360°F/180°C	10
Banana Bread	360°F/180°C	30
Cookies	360°F/180°C	10
Cupcakes	360°F/180°C	10
Doughnuts	360°F/180°C	15
Fruit Crumble	360°F/180°C	15
Mug Cakes	360°F/180°C	15

III. Potato Air Frying

	Temperature	Time(Minutes)
French Fries	360°F/180°C	25
Sweet Potatoes	360°F/180°C	15
Curly Fries	360°F/180°C	15
Jacket Potatoes	360°F/180°C	20

Index/Recipe Index

Guide: ***ONLY*** Recipes Index is in Upper Case.

A

acrylamide, 14, 21, 22
AIR ROASTED ASPARAGUS, 115
APPLE DUMPLINGS, 175
ARTICHOKE HEARTS, 139
ASIAN SALMON, 93
AVOCADO FRIES, 121
Avocadoes, 195

B

BACON-WRAPPED SHRIMP, 78
BAKED BANANA BREAD, 171
BAKED SALMON, 88
bananas, 171, 172
BANG BANG FRIED SHRIMP, 73
BEEF AND BROCCOLI, 186
breadcrumbs, 13, 104, 107, 117, 137, 138, 139, 147, 156, 178, 190, 191
BREADED MUSHROOMS, 190
BUFFALO CAULIFLOWER, 117
BUFFALO CHICKEN MEATBALLS, 156
buffalo sauce, 118, 156
Bundt Pans, 25
butter mixture, 178
BUTTERMILK FRIED CHICKEN, 152

C

Cabbages, 195
CAJUN SALMON, 91
CAJUN SHRIMP, 75
cancer, 8, 21, 22
Cantaloupes, 195
Cauliflower, 5, 95, 112, 117, 195
celery, 157
Celery, 195
Cherries, 195
CHICKEN FAJITA DINNER, 150
CHICKEN WINGS 'N' SAUCE, 144
Chocolate Sauce, 6, 167
CHURROS WITH CHOCOLATE SAUCE, 165
CILANTRO LIME SHRIMP SKEWERS, 83
cinnamon, 165, 166, 173, 179
CINNAMON APPLE CHIPS WITH ALMOND YOGURT DIP, 173
CINNAMON TOAST, 179
clover honey, 160
COCONUT SHRIMP WITH DIPPING SAUCE, 71
Cosori 3.7 Quart Air Fryer, 34
CRISPY BROCCOLI, 119
CRISPY EGGPLANT PARMESAN, 137
CRISPY KALE CHIPS, 133
CRISPY ROASTED BRUSSELS SPROUTS, 131
CRUMBED FISH, 101

D

Deep frying, 14
dough, 166, 169, 176
DOUGHNUTS, 168

F

FISH CAKE RECIPE, 103
FRIED CATFISH, 108
FRIED GREEN TOMATOES, 134
FRIED STEAK, 182
frozen food, 50, 51, 52
frozen vegetables, 55, 111

G

GARLIC MUSHROOMS, 187
GARLIC PARMESAN SHRIMP, 69
GoWISE USA 5.5 Liters Air Fryer, 35
Grapes, 195
Greek yogurt, 173
Grill Pan, 26
GRILLED FISH FILLET WITH PESTO SAUCE, 106

H

Hasselback Potato Slicing Rack, 27
HONEY GARLIC CHICKEN WINGS, 160
HONEY MUSTARD CHICKEN BREASTS, 158
HONEY ROASTED CARROTS, 136
HONEY SRIRACHA SALMON, 90
Honeydew, 195

I

Instant Meat and Food Thermometer, 28
International Cancer Research Agency, 21

K

Kale, 6, 113, 133, 195
ketogenic, 9
Kiwis, 195

L

LEMON GARLIC SALMON, 86
LEMON GARLIC SHRIMP, 65
LEMON PEPPER SHRIMP, 67

M

Maillard reactions, 14
Mushrooms, 7, 113, 195

N

National Cancer Institute (NCI), 22
Nectarines, 195

O

obesity, 20
Oil Sprayers, 23
OMORC 6 Quart Air Fryer, 35

P

PANKO BREADED CHICKEN PARMESAN WITH MARINARA SAUCE, 146
papayas, 195
paper liners, 29
Pears, 195
PINEAPPLE CAKE, 177
Pineapples, 195
POPCORN SHRIMP, 81
PORK CHOP, 189
PORK LOIN, 184
potato starch, 160

S

SALMON & ASPARAGUS, 97

SALMON AND CAULIFLOWER RICE BOWLS, 95
SATAY CHICKEN SKEWERS, 154
SHISHITO PEPPERS WITH LIME, 141
Skewer, 154
Spinach, 195
stir, 11, 84, 96, 132, 166, 167, 169, 178
Strawberries, 195
Sweet Corn, 195
SWEET POTATO FRIES, 123

T

TANDOORI SALMON, 99
Tomatoes, 6, 114, 195
TURKEY BREAST, 162
TURKEY BREAST RECIPE WITH LEMON PEPPER, 148

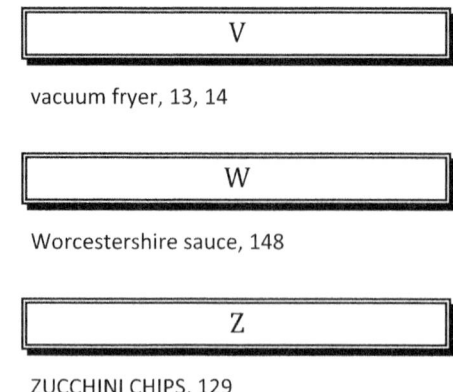

V

vacuum fryer, 13, 14

W

Worcestershire sauce, 148

Z

ZUCCHINI CHIPS, 129
ZUCCHINI FRIES, 127
ZUCCHINI, YELLOW SQUASH, AND CARROTS, 125

Printed in Great Britain
by Amazon